The Magical World of Burlesque

1973 – 1986

By
Dusty Summers

∞ INFINITY PUBLISHING

Copyright © 2013 by Dusty Summers

ISBN 978-0-7414-9874-8 Paperback
ISBN 978-0-7414-9875-5 eBook
Library of Congress Control Number: 2013916940

Printed in the United States of America

Published September 2014

INFINITY PUBLISHING
1094 New DeHaven Street, Suite 100
West Conshohocken, PA 19428-2713
Toll-free (877) BUY BOOK
Local Phone (610) 941-9999
Fax (610) 941-9959
Info@buybooksontheweb.com
www.buybooksontheweb.com

Acknowledgements

I was encouraged to write this book by my fans and my family. Kitten Natividad gave me a final push in a note telling me to "go for it." My daughters Catherine Taber and Angel Brock and husband Ken Burrows helped with the proofreading. Angel also assisted me with some of the photos. Justin Fernandez gave me encouragement and welcome suggestions.

Most of the photos in the book are from my own collection. In a few cases, I had to ask the people I wrote about for a copy of the photos in my articles. My thanks go to Carme Petrillo, Georgette Dante, and Brandon Scott.

My husband's generosity made this book possible. He is truly "the wind beneath my wings!"

This book would not be possible if not for the entertainers who shared their stories with me years ago and those who brought me up to date on their lives today.

I sincerely appreciate the efforts of Jenny Lee and Dixie Evans who have helped keep burlesque alive through Exotic World now known as The Burlesque Hall of Fame.

I am so grateful to the burlesque world for bringing me back to the stage. It is a bit like being reborn!

The cover photo is from my performance at Burlesque Hall of Fame in 2009 and was taken by Ed Barnes. The back cover photo is from my performance at Burlesque Hall of Fame in 2013 and was taken by Thomas Hoffman.

Foreword

I have been a performer since 1966, starting out as a bikini go-go dancer at the Airline Inn in Phoenix, Arizona. Less than a year later I performed in a burlesque revival attempt at a theatre in downtown Phoenix, starring Monkey Kirkland. (My parent's used to go to Guys and Dolls in Phoenix and see Monkey Kirkland when I was a kid)! In 1971 I would work with Monkey in New York City at the Follies Burlesque Theater. Monkey was the stereotype of a burlesque comic, short, dumpy, red faced and funny as hell!

Except for that short lived burlesque revival show, there wasn't any burlesque in Arizona, so I kind of made it up as I went, inspired mostly by the movie "Gypsy" an overly glamorous look at burlesque but, nevertheless, my inspiration. I was one of the few go-go dancers in Phoenix who was allowed, even encouraged to dance slow and sexy when the trend was the wild rock and roll shimmying of go-go girls on small stages set up usually next to the bandstand. Most were barely wide enough to take two steps forward and two steps back.

I would come down off the little stage and hit the main dance floor, swaying and dancing to tunes like: "Moon River," " Hello Dolly," "Fever," "Big Spender," anything bluesy or romantic. Many of the numbers would eventually make their way into my strip routines. Don't get me wrong though. I could shake my booty with the best of them. I landed my first job in 1966 at the Airline Inn in Phoenix auditioning to Sandy Nelson's "Let There Be Drums."

I didn't have the advantage of a mentor so I studied dance moves I liked from musicals on television and from other dancers I worked with over the years. A little here, a little there, but with my own personal stamp or stomp as it might have looked in the beginning! Even Chris Star, a burlesque star in the 1950's, who was the choreographer for the old time burlesque revival show in Phoenix, did not teach me to strip. She taught me the steps I needed to learn for the chorus line, which is where I started. A couple of weeks later, all the features, the singer, and most of the chorus line were cut from the show due to sparse audiences. That left five of us in the chorus line, only now we were in the chorus line AND we had to do a strip routine, which was to be a different routine each week. I started out as Little Egypt with a borrowed costume from Chris Star. Since we weren't told of our "promotion" until the day before, there was no rehearsal of our strips. The first time I danced to "Little Egypt" I fumbled trying to find the right hook and eyes to remove the layers of veils. I was the clumsiest Egyptian enticer ever seen on a burlesque stage!

When the theatre closed a few weeks later, I took my "act" on the road and was the star at The Body Shop and the Airport Inn in Tucson. When I returned to Phoenix a few months later, it was back to go-go but I retained my "stripper moves" fitting them in whenever I could.

I felt a bit like an ice skater, as I slid smoothly across the stage, with a bit of a dip, a wink, a smile, and a bump or two, all in the most lady-like way I could.

How I wanted to be elegant like Natalie Wood! At five feet, two inches, elegant was probably a bit of a reach! However, I loved the movement of dance, the smiles from the customers, and oh how I loved the applause.

My road to burlesque stardom was slow and steady. I was first a featured go-go dancer at places like the Airline Inn and the HiLiter in Phoenix in (1966), the Bat Cave in Hollywood, California (1967), Sonny's and the Dinner Bell in Portland, Oregon (1968). I was the featured exotic at the Hubba Hubba in Honolulu in 1968. When performing in California, Oregon, and Arizona, I often combined go-go dancing and burlesque.

After the birth of my daughters, Angel in 1969, and Catherine in 1970, I decided to hell with go-go, I needed to stick with stripping which was much easier on me physically. It was time to become a burlesque star!

I was the co-feature exotic at Guys and Dolls in Phoenix (1972), and the featured exotic at the Camelback Lounge and the Tender Trap in Phoenix (1973).

In Boston at the Teddy Bear Lounge (1973), I started out as a co-feature and became the feature. I was the feature at the Stage Door in Buffalo, New York (1972), Frank Gay's Marquee in Rockford, Illinois (1972), Victory Burlesk Theatre in Toronto, Canada (1972), the Palace Theatrical Club in Wheeling, West Virginia (1972), the Golden Banana in Peabody, Massachusetts as well as the Squires in Revere Beach, Massachusetts (1980), Hannah's in Savannah, Georgia, (1975), and the Penthouse in Vancouver, Canada (1981) just to name a few. I featured at clubs all over Florida including Surfside 7 in Ft. Walton Beach in 1974 and again in 1980 (a more complete list can be found at the end of this book). Along the path, I met

so many beautiful dancers, funny comics, club owners, fans, and oh yes, nine husbands!!!

I especially enjoyed performing in the old burlesque skits with Monkey Kirkland and Ralph Clifford at the Follies Burlesque in New York City in 1972. I worked with Art Watts and Gene Vaughan at the Capri Art Burlesk Theatre in Memphis in 1973. In 1977 I got the chance to do more burlesque skits with Bob Mitchell, Charlie Vespia at the Royal Las Vegas in 1975 and again at the Maxim Hotel in 1979.

I worked with some of the funniest comics in burlesque including comic/magician Professor Turban (whom I met and married in Ft. Walton Beach, Florida in 1974), and Artie Brooks at the Palomino in North Las Vegas. I worked with Johnny Burgess at the Cork Club in Cocoa Beach, Florida and again at Surfside 7 in Ft. Walton Beach. I booked legendary comics Jimmy Matthews and Dexter Maitland in San Angelo, Texas at my own club Dusty's West as well as Professor Turban about ten years after our divorce! Johnny Burgess also worked for me at Dusty's West.

This book features edited columns I wrote for various newspapers in Las Vegas, Nevada, Phoenix, Arizona, Ft. Walton Beach, Florida, and San Angelo, Texas. Some of the performers I wrote on more than once and in more than one city!

In 2006, Kitten Natividad told Paula the Swedish Housewife to give me a call about doing the Exotic World show to be held in downtown Las Vegas at the Celebrity Theatre. At the time I was up in Sturgis, South Dakota. "Would I come and do a show for the four-day burlesque festival?" Paula asked.

She assured me that I wouldn't have to take anything off. Maybe I could do some magic? I reluctantly agreed, mostly because my niece was getting married that same weekend at Mount Charleston and I could do the Exotic World show on Friday and go to her wedding on Saturday. A few days later I flew to Las Vegas and met Paula at the theater.

"Oh my God, you're beautiful!" she said as she ran forward to meet me. No one had said that to me in years and certainly not with the kind of enthusiasm Paula did. She asked me for my music CD. CD? My music was on cassette tapes. Times had changed and I was about to discover just how much they changed.

It was a whirlwind weekend, meeting and greeting all the "neo burlesquers" and so many of the women I'd worked with in the past. Others I had heard of through the years because I saw their signatures on dressing room walls or I followed them into a nightclub or theatre or saw their photos posted as "coming attraction."

In 2005, my husband Ken and I were given a guided tour through the Exotic World Museum in Helendale, California by Dixie Evans, "The Marilyn Monroe of Burlesque." Dixie, a burlesque star from the 1950's, was brimming with energy and was delighted to show us the thousands of pieces of burlesque memorabilia including props, costumes, photos, newspaper clippings, and books on burlesque. She gave us a history of the museum telling us how Jenny Lee had started it in the 1950's and since 1990 after Jenny's death; it had been in Dixie Evan's capable hands. Jenny Lee and Dixie Evans have managed to preserve the art, the history, and the culture of the burlesque art form.

Before 2006, I didn't know burlesque was back. The Exotic World Festival, now known as Burlesque Hall

of Fame, was and is all part of the burlesque revival. The yearly show grows bigger and bigger and is the main fund raising event supporting the Burlesque Hall of Fame Museum now located in downtown Las Vegas in the Emergency Arts Building on Fremont Street across from the El Cortez Hotel.

I have performed in the Burlesque Hall of Fame Festival every year since 2006. I am enjoying the burlesque renaissance and hope it never ends! I am amazed at the sharing of information, burlesque instruction, the love, and the support that these new burlesquers show for each other and for us even gracing us with the title of "Legend." Sounds a lot better than over-the-hill stripper!

Many of the columns in this book have been posted on my Facebook page eliciting lots of "likes" and requests for more. In July of 2013, I posted a story on Kitten Natividad and Delilah Jones and asked my readers would they be interested in a book containing all of my columns. I was delighted at the response. Within an hour I received 80 or 90 "likes" dozens of posts, and lots of email all encouraging me to share these columns.

I hope you enjoy this look at the burlesque performers from the '60's, '70's and 80's. If you get a chance to meet any of them, have them sign your book. History is valuable for the knowledge and even more valuable autographed!

NOTE: Names of performers who have photos in this book are capitalized and in bold print. Some of the exact dates of the columns were lost during numerous moves and they are listed by year only.

Come Together

Note: The Come Together columns were published in Phoenix, Arizona, where I lived, while I was on tour.

1973 It seems fitting in my first column to start by answering the first question I am usually asked by members of the audience. Why are you a dancer?

I started dancing seven short years ago, at the Airline Inn in Phoenix, when I answered an ad for go-go girls wanted. I'd never even seen a go-go girl but it sounded glamorous.

I was hired immediately at $2.50 an hour. I couldn't believe the high wages and for doing something I liked!

I've had the opportunity for traveling all over the USA and Canada at wages up to $600 a week, meeting celebrities (yes, they like us too), meeting politicians and seeing places and doing things I could not possibly do on a secretaries $80 a week salary.

An audience, of course, isn't always kind. Sometimes they pick you apart, especially the women with comments such as: "I've got more than that!" Most audiences just want to be entertained and so we enjoy each other.

It is true some girls do it only for the money. You'll usually find the girl who is making the best money is also the one who really likes entertaining. After all, you try harder when you like what

you're doing.

It is rare to find a girl who dances only because she wants to show off her body. Most of us are very self-conscious of our looks in general and our bodies in particular. There isn't much you can hide under bright lights and even small imperfections seem like major disfigurements on stage.

It is also true that a few girls dance in order to meet men. In reality however, dancing is a job and as such occupies a great deal of prime dating time, such as holidays and Friday and Saturday nights.

One common misconception is that dancers are hookers. It isn't necessary to work your rump off as a dancer if your intention is to lie on it for money. How much is a weary rump worth?

Finally, it is not true that dancers dance only because they can't do anything else. You'd be surprised at the number of secretaries, sales ladies, waitresses, bookkeepers and even schoolteachers who supplement their income by dancing. In fact, in one club I worked, the HiLiter in Phoenix, all the members of the band were Arizona State University graduates, the bartender was working on a PhD, and every dancer except one attended either ASU or Phoenix College. The exception was a stewardess!

Come Together

1973 Here I am again coming to you direct from Waverly, Iowa. "Where's Waverly?" you ask. About 30 miles from Mason City, Iowa. It's close to Bremer, Readlyn and Waterloo. In other words, I never heard of it either.

Waverly has a population of just

over 7,000 people, which doesn't mean too much. Just as in California, most of the towns in Iowa are next-door neighbors or part of the suburbs to bigger cities, in this case, Mason City.

Sir Lounge is the only club for many miles offering exotic entertainment. It is a beautiful club with simulated knights of armor décor.

I work with an exotic dancer here billed as Vampira. One of her shows is centered around a casket!

Her most clever show, I thought, entailed one audience participant whom she dressed in an ape costume. During her last number, "Harry the Hairy Ape," the ape comes on the stage and dances with her and then carries her off to the dressing room. It looks very realistic.

When she's not being Vampira, she is called Lynn and is a very cute Gemini. A dancer for seven years, she does her own bookings and has several variety shows including an Indian fire show and a Spanish show.

An interesting dish served at a restaurant next to my motel is called "Calorie Counter Continental Wieners $1.80." That's a mighty fancy name for cheese stuffed hot dogs!

Come Together

1973 As every customer will verify and as every entertainer will agree, a complete show enhanced by lively personalities and a whole lot of talent makes a beautiful fast-paced evening. Such has been the case this week at Surfside 7 in Fort Walton Beach, Florida.

Leading our show off every evening is **PROFESSOR TURBAN**. He immediately gets the audience relaxed and in a friendly mood with some beautifully timed jokes and some quick magic to lead you later in the show through several more difficult and dramatic tricks.

Then, as in Phoenix, I do my usual show. Actually, except for some more wardrobe and some new music, my show is pretty much as you remember it. And I do hope you remember it.

Opening the show is **MISS GINA MONIQUE**, a petite brunette who bounces on stage to some sexy saxophone music. She moves across the stage seductively and gracefully. Gina has a bubbly smile on her face all the time, the kind of smile that makes customers wonder, "just what is she thinking?"

CHARAE whirls out on the stage next, dressed in a gypsy costume of beautiful pink veils, dancing to every song ever written about a gypsy. She also has a wild fire show done to the tune of "I Am the God of Hellfire." And, as if this were not enough, you would think you were back in Arizona when she comes out dressed as an Indian with enough feathers to equip a whole tribe.

Usually at about this point in the show, Professor Turban produces two live doves from a flaming frying pan, unhooks and rehooks some solid unhookable rings, and tosses away a pack of cards from nowhere, all to some lively comedy. His magic and comedy go together like Victor Borge's piano and comedy.

Completing this week's show is **MISS GALAXIE**. She makes her entrance via the rhythmic clicking of Latin castanets. What I think the audience is really waiting for is a peek at her ample 44D bosom. And, as with any girl amply endowed, you can hear the same whispered question all over the audience. "Are they real?" Galaxie assures you they are, indeed, real.

Come Together

1973 The light this week is on **MISS GALAXIE** (pictured), 44D-23-36, who is appearing at Surfside 7 in Ft. Walton Beach, Florida. Galaxie does a lively show to the clicking of castanets in a Latin version strip. She urges her audience to join in the beat by clapping their hands.

Galaxie is a college graduate, former circus performer, animal trainer and a top exotic performer. She is from Wiesbaden, West Germany where she graduated from Obershule University as a teacher. However, the lure of the Shrine Circus drew her into its web and she remained with it, traveling throughout Europe for several years.

She performed acrobatic wire stunts, including one that I've seen a few times on television. She also rode a motorcycle on a tight rope! Her animal training was all done in the circus where she primarily trained elephants and tigers. Galaxie preferred training tigers but "they were mean s.o.b.'s."

In 1963, Galaxie came to the U. S. where she became a naturalized citizen in 1967. She arrived in New York City and started her career as an exotic dancer at the Broadway Theatre in Manhattan. Galaxie has since featured in some of the top clubs in America, including Three Stars in Tulsa, T-Bone in Wichita, and the Idle Hour in Anchorage. She was also a part of the Minsky's revue in Las Vegas.

Miss Galaxie is single with a three-year-old daughter. I asked her what kind of a man she was looking for and she replied, "an employed gentleman." That certainly says it well. If anyone is interested in dating Galaxie, she enjoys tennis and golfing.

Come Together

1974 **CHARAE** (pictured), is a 23 year old ex schoolteacher turned exotic appearing at Surfside 7 in Ft. Walton Beach, Florida. Making her home in Orlando, Florida, Charae has traveled all over the mid-west and the south in her year as an exotic.

Her measurements, 36-24-35, are well proportioned on a 124 lb., 5'9" frame. Her long blonde hair and brown eyes help to captivate her audience.

Charae graduated from the University of Iowa with a teacher's degree in psychology. She spent one year in a high school as a student teacher. "I love kids and I love teaching, but at the high school level, they get to be smart-alecks and when I found myself wanting to pop one of them I decided that teaching wasn't for me."

Two well-known names in the exotic field, Rita Atlanta and Miss Hollywood, started Charae on her way as an exotic dancer. Charae performs theme shows as well as a straight strip. She has a fire show, a gypsy show, and a wild Indian show. She enjoys her theme shows "because they are different. I am a sensationalist and I like to do shows that make people sit back and take stock, whether they do or not."

Charae also plays the organ and guitar and at one time performed with a band called The Jokers. How did she fit so much activity into 23 years? "I graduated high school at 15 because I skipped two years of grade school," she replied. Now who was that who said "dumb blondes?"

Some of the clubs Charae has especially enjoyed working in include:

Cheetah II in Half Day, Illinois, Vagabond in Chicago, and the Paradise in Appleton, Wisconsin. She would eventually like to own her own club, "a supper club with show bands and I already have it picked out in Orlando."

With her qualifications and self-confidence, I have no doubt that Charae will be operating that club very soon.

NOTE: Charae taught me how to do fire.

Come Together

1974 The lovely girl pictured here is **GINA MONIQUE,** a 5'2" brunette with measurements of 35-24½-35½. She is a former housewife turned exotic.

Gina, who is from the small town of Beatrice, Nebraska, has traveled all over the U.S. in her three years as an exotic. She has performed in many of the biggest nightclubs including the Midway Lounge in Pittsburg, the Pink Pussy Cat in Rochester, New York and Club Juana in Orlando.

I asked Gina what makes a mother, with two daughters age two and four, become an exotic. She replied, "I am a stripper because I make good money and I don't have to work hard."

Gina does not, however, intend to make entertainment her permanent career. "I want to dance part-time and go to school part time to be a doctor. I think I'll be either a general practioner or a gynecologist."

As with most entertainers, Gina has had her embarrassing moments on stage. She relates the following: "It was my second engagement at the Midway Lounge in Pittsburg. My first show of the night I had a beautiful new prop with lights all around it and covered in felt. As soon as I laid down on it, it fell to the floor! I just slid it to the side and used a chair to finish my show."

Gina's hobbies include painting and jazz music. Sorry guys, Gina is wrapped up right now with a jazz musician.

She would like to go west to perform so maybe some of you in Arizona will have the opportunity to see a vivacious, charming woman in the person of Gina Monique.

As It Is!

Note: As It Is columns were included in my own entertainment newspaper, published in Ft. Walton Beach, Florida, where I made my home after marrying Professor Turban.

December 12, 1974 Trader Jon's in Pensacola, Florida is many things in one club, a historical museum, a photograph gallery and a burlesque room. All of this is run by one of the town's most beloved and infamous characters – Trader Jon.

Trader, as he is called, puts in unbelievable hours at his club, starting at 9 or 9:30 in the morning and going full-guns until 2:30AM. Sixty years young, many a teenager would envy the get up and go of this cheerful man.

The walls of Trader Jon's are decorated in photographs of Navy men and Blue Angels of which Trader is a certified member, in fact, he still retains his pilot's license. Hanging from the ceiling are homemade model airplanes, some of them nearly big enough to fly! Scattered throughout the club are enough Navy mementos to outfit a small naval fleet.

Chairs at the rickety wooden bar are comfortable over-sized barber chairs. On the floor, metal ice cream parlor chairs are seated around an array of tables made from sewing machine cabinets, picnic benches and other tables – modes that you could spend hours trying to figure out. One of the booths is made from the brass iron frame of a bed. Bits of rope and net hanging from the ceiling give the customer the challenge of an obstacle course as he tries to find his way to a table.

Live entertainment is featured in the persons of **TURBAN**, well-known Miracle Strip magician and his partner, **DUSTY SUMMERS**, with her popular cowboy magic show featuring a fire dance to "Ring of Fire." The extraordinarily agile Linda Star is also featured.

As It Is!

December 19, 1974 Offering the finest in burlesque, six nights a week, is Carmichael's Surfside Seven near the Shalimar Bridge in Ft. Walton Beach, Florida.

The lively show is presently featuring **CASEY JONES**, "The Baby Doll of Burlesque" (pictured), in her baby doll show. She also has a cute railroad engineer show complete with a locomo-tive. Also featured are Tiffany and Bobbie Lynn.

Tiffany, the girl with the all-American college look, entertains her audience with a sophisticated show including a special French maid number.

The blonde loveliness of Bobbie Lynn completes the all-star line –up.

Be sure and catch the daytime "peek-a-boo-review" starting at 5PM daily with some of Florida's top go-go dancers.

The Prince of Magic has appeared on the Miracle Strip in various nightspots the last ten years as **PROFESSOR TURBAN**, Prince of Magic (pictured). He has entertained residents and visitors with his magic, comedy and singing and now he will be the star of his own TV Show for Channel 6 entitled "The Land of the Enchanted Forest," co-starring his wife The Princess of Magic, **DUSTY SUMMERS.**

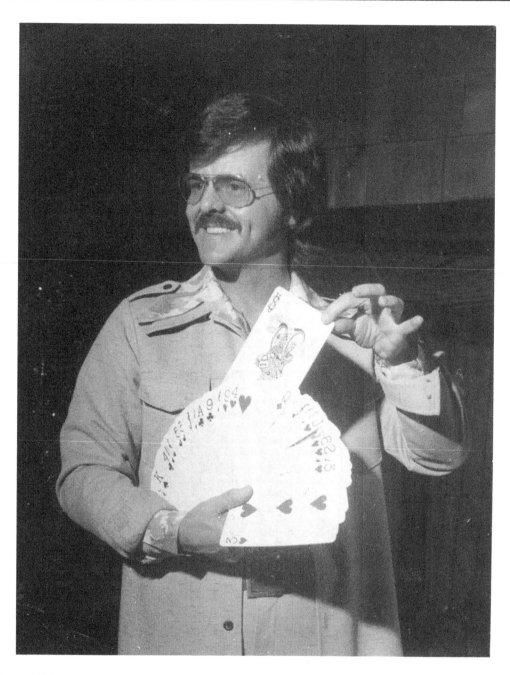

In addition to his nightclub work, Turban has always been available for charitable fund drives, lending his talent to get people to dig down and give to some worthy cause. The last two years it was the Cancer Marathon for Chanel 6 and a Muscular Dystrophy Benefit at Grants.

Monday, he gave a special show to the Gulf Convalescent Home for the older folks. Turban says, "These are beautiful people and all too often are forgotten at this festive time of the year. I believe that advancing age does not affect one's ability to laugh and be mystified."

A mark of the truly versatile performer is his ability to entertain all age groups and people from all walks of life. Before coming to Florida, Turban had another children's TV show in Topeka, Kansas called "Turban's Land of

Magic." He also made a three year tour of schools in the Midwest giving two or three shows a day to packed school auditoriums.

Turban has toured the country with the Inkspots performing one-night stands at nightclubs, theaters, schools, and concert halls. He has also appeared with such stars as Brenda Lee, the Four Freshman and the original Emmett Kelly.

Turban co-starred in a not yet shown TV pilot movie "Down Under" starring Dennis Weaver, presently of the "McCloud" series. Turban jokingly says, "By the time "McCloud" is over, they'll have to find a younger man to take my place!"

He also appeared in "One More Chance" which starred Sammy Davis Jr. and Peter Lawford.

His present plans include the weekly TV series for Channel 6, some promotional work for shopping centers, land development openings and other publicity work.

As It Is!

December 1974 In the eleven years Jeannie Thomas (pictured) has been an entertainer, she has managed to play the top nightspots in and out of the country.

Combining her exotic talents with a strong vibrant voice, she is in the $1000 a week class, which is hard to reach in any field.

Although Jeannie has retired from the exotic field to sing with the band Cornbread, now playing at Bacons by the Sea, she still performs her special fire show nightly in G-string and pasties.

"The nudity is necessary to prevent going up in flames," she says. "I call the show bathing my body in fire and I perform it to "2001 Space Odyssey." It seems to go over well."

Jeannie likes to sing torch, blues and ballads. Currently she gets a lot of requests for "Angie Baby" and other Helen Reddy material. She also performs Bobbie Gentry and she likes Streisand but she says there is not much call for it.

Some of the highlight performances of Jeannie's career were her appearances at the Cabaret in Las Vegas, the Follies in New York City, and singing with Dave Burton at the Thunderbird in Las Vegas. She also did a show for the USS Saratoga before it went to Vietnam.

Her exceptional beauty lent itself to television commercials for Hamilton washers and dryers and for Maybelline. She even did some bit parts in the horror movie "Creature of the Lagoon."

Jeannie is proud of her Cherokee Indian heritage. As an exotic, she had an authentic Cherokee Indian show, complete with an elegant chief's headdress.

Entertaining comes naturally to Jeannie. She explains, "I just started picking it up and doing it."

Jeannie attended nursing school at Purdue University. She also received an AA in business and graduated from beauty college. With Jeannie's phenomenal success, you can see that she graduated from the school of experience magna cum laude!

As It Is!

January 9, 1975 I thought maybe for those of you who don't have the opportunity to travel and see dancers in other parts of the country, you might be interested in just how much or how little of the dancers you can see.

Most of us think of Boston as a puritan, Victorian city. Boston has a section of downtown called the "Combat Zone" and in it are a multitude of X-rated movie houses, strip clubs, masseuse parlors, porno book stores, tattoo artists, and so on.

On the Boston law books it was once stated that girls could not remove their clothes on stage - - so the girls simply went off the stage, removed their clothes and came back to dance. Presently, Boston dancers must strip all the way. Many of their clubs are known for b-drinking and prostitution as well. B-drinking is the practice of girls making commissions from drinks they "persuade" customers to buy for them. Some clubs pressure girls to increase drink sales and many of the girls make more money in commissions than they make for performing.

In Grand Rapids, Michigan, dancers must wear net bras and pasties but they can strip down to a G-string.

In Washington D.C., another heavy b-drinking city, dancers can strip to G-strings and pasties but they cannot touch the floor with anything but their feet. They may not touch their bodies either, except to remove something.

In Portland, Oregon, the law is pasties and G-strings but strippers can only work where food is served! Actually, all cocktail licenses must be coupled with food.

Cedar Rapids, Iowa and Phoenix, Arizona require net bras, pasties, and full panties at least three inches wide in back. Phoenix also requires hose. Who checks the three inches? The friendly vice cops, of course, whom you can quickly identify by the ruler poking out of his back pocket!

If you visit Ft. Wayne, Indiana, stay awhile. The laws there change every few weeks.

California, famous for its nudity, has a wide variety of laws from city to city. In Los Angeles the girls were recently ordered to cover up—completely. But some enterprising ice cream parlors now offer nudity with your sundaes! Apparently, the dairy industry featuring nudity is wholesome, where as nudity and booze are not.

In Richmond, Virginia and in Huntsville, Alabama, the girls must wear pasties but the law doesn't specify what kind, so the girls wear clear tape.

In Toledo, Ohio, the law states G-strings must be worn and the elastic must show. However, the law doesn't state the G-string has to cover anything so . . . you guessed it, the girls just wear the elastic strings!

The ingenuity award goes to an Orangevale, California club. Court was actually held in a nightclub, The Pink Pussycat, to determine if nude dancing was obscene. The jury watched a complete nude review, applauded loudly, and then voted it obscene. The law then stated the girls could not perform nude on stage.

The enterprising club owner rigged up closed circuit cameras in the back room and as each girl's turn to dance came up, she would go in the back room, strip and dance before the cameras and the customers watched her on TV!

UPDATE: Laws continually change everywhere. They are set by each city and each county and may differ greatly. Las Vegas, for one, has laws that differ from one side of the street to the other!

As It Is!

January 30, 1975 I have been asked numerous times: "Why did you become a stripper? What are you doing in a place like this?"

As with many of today's exotic dancers, I started out as a go-go dancer. My first job was in a small neighborhood cocktail lounge where I worked six days a week, five hours a day at the unbelievable salary of $2.50 an hour. A side benefit of my job was the welcome loss of nearly ten pounds in the first two weeks.

I found that I enjoyed the challenge of spontaneous creativity, expressing feelings through dance and making up new steps to new songs. I also enjoyed the applause and the smiles of the customers I performed for. Most of the customers were men but there were many couples too.

From go-go dancing, I went into chorus line work and back to go-go dancing and then into exotic dancing. I've heard many patrons of the clubs I've worked express the opinion that all a dancer has to do is "shake her a . . . and take off her clothes. Anyone can do that!"

Well anyone CAN do that. But that is far from all there is to it. In order to earn a steady wage, in my case up to $600 a week, there is a lot of preparation and thought given to my shows.

A show is approximately 20 minutes. I choose my music in tempos not only geared to removing my clothes without falling on my face, but to entertain and keep the audience awake, and to create a theme.

I also choose my costumes with the same thoughts in mind. Since I make my own, this is not too difficult to do but it does require a lot of time. Things I look for in a costume are sex appeal for the men AND for the women (a burlesque show is often a fashion show for female customers), ease of removal, and the ability to express the show theme.

An exotic dancer's wardrobe can also be considered a prop much as a typist's typewriter or a mechanic's tools. They are designed to do a job and in order to do it well; they must be kept in excellent order.

Since a dancer inevitably gets down to the skin, there is the body to be considered. I am extremely conscious of diet, exercise, make-up and hair.

As with many exotics, I've added a few gimmick touches to my shows. I have a western show in which I perform a fire dance and yes, sometimes I DO get burned. I have several shows in which I incorporate magic such as when I dance with a beautiful white dove in each hand and make them vanish or when Professor Turban, my partner, produces me from an empty basket.

These touches add interest to what would normally be a straight strip and give people something to talk about.

So far as the actual exhibiting of my body, I do not feel that any dancer can rely on that alone to entertain. We are all extremely self-conscious of every flaw. Some members of the audience seem to get their jollies by pointing them out, so reliance on nudity alone is simply not enough. Very few dancers have perfect bodies. We simply use what we have, the best we can.

I've often heard the comment that exotics are a dying art – a passing phase. Can any of us remember when viewing a graceful female body did not exist? As long as there are women and men, there will be exotic dancers. It is one line of work in which there is no material shortage and there is always consumer interest!

Vegas Visitor

Note: These articles were published in my column The Magical World of Burlesque. I began writing them about a year after I decided to make Las Vegas home.

January 23, 1977 My first Las Vegas column starts out with my grateful appreciation to my co-workers in burlesque for their generosity and kindness during my recent emergency surgery and convalescence.

At the Palomino, where I appear in the nighttime show, all the employees donated money to help me. At the same time, a collection was taken up for me at the Cabaret and at the Royal Las Vegas.

While in the hospital, I received lots of calls, cards, and beautiful flowers and even more importantly a visit from each performer working with me at the Palomino. That's right, each performer and the light man too!

It has been said that you never know who your real friends are until you get into trouble. I'm almost glad I got ill, I feel so good!

In this column, you will find the

latest news in the burlesque field as well as reviews of other shows about town as I see them. I hope you enjoy them. Again, thank-you friends!

I've been writing since grade school when I composed mini-fairy tales inside the covers of my geography book. I've written entertainment columns in Phoenix, Arizona and more recently in Ft. Walton Beach, Florida, and I've been the publisher of my own entertainment magazine. I enjoy telling people what's going on in the most exciting business of them all, entertainment.

Currently, I recommend **GEORGETTE DANTE**, in the "Rare and Bare" revue, at the Royal Las Vegas for the most unusual and daring exotic act in the business. She twirls fire tassels, blows fire, carries one or more customers across her shoulders as she twirls them round and round and then she carries them back to their seats. Then she goes into the audience and teaches customers to eat fire while she is busy picking their pockets!

You'll find comedy with **ARTIE BROOKS** at the Guys and Dolls. A Don Rickles-type comic, he is never at a loss for a comeback to a heckler.

Enjoy the most beautiful girls in burlesque plus the magic and comedy of

TURBAN, Prince of Magic at the Cabaret. Turban produces an array of cards, silks and doves, as he tickles your funny bone.

The Amateur Nude Dance Contest is still going strong at the world famous Palomino Club. Emceed by the very funny **BOB MITCHELL**, the contest features lots of young ladies competing nightly for cash prizes. The contest is in addition to the professional burlesque show that starts daily at 2PM and goes on to about 4:30 in the morning.

Finally, I recommend Jackie Gayle at the Casbar Lounge in the Sahara. On a recent Tuesday night during the "slow season," the lounge was packed with laughing patrons. A quick wit and a wealth of comic material have made Jackie Gayle a lively one-man show.

Following him was "Pin Ups '77", a fantastic show combining the dancing talents of the Pin Ups and the singing of Mary Welch plus the comedy of Peter Anthony.

I was especially impressed with Mary Welch. She has an energetic lifting delivery and is a superb impersonator doing a hilarious takeoff on Mae West. She outdoes Natalie Cole on the hit record "Mr. Melody." Keep an eye on this girl. She's going places.

Vegas Visitor

February 4, 1977 If burlesque is your favorite way to be entertained, then Las Vegas is certainly the place to be. We have a large variety of classy clubs featuring the top exotics in the world.

The Guys and Dolls is currently featuring "Miss Nude Universe, **KITTEN NATIVIDAD** (pictured). Her body certainly tells you why she won the title but just winning a title doesn't

necessarily make you a good act. Kitten, however, is one of the best I've seen. She literally bubbles on stage, bathing her nude body in a revolving clear bowl of suds on stage and laughingly shaking the excess suds and water all over the ringside audience. Kitten has the talent to put across a sensual show without a hint of vulgarity.

Killer-miss nude universe

Also on the same bill is another gorgeous body, **MISS DIERDRE RHODES**. A couple of years ago, Dierdre entered a Miss Nude Universe contest and placed fourth in the contest and won the title of Miss Nude Photogenic. On stage, Dierdre is a picture of grace and femininity. Not only that, but the lady can dance!

LIBERTY WEST (pictured) is the co-feature of the show and again another dynamite body. She has the most controlled pectoral muscles in town. She can move her assets in any direction and in any position.

LIBERTY WEST

Continental (International) Theatrical Agency, Lt
P. O. BOX 007, GAYS MILLS, WIS. 54631
PHONE (608) 624-3277

Pandora, from Washington D.C., is a relative newcomer to the stage, but is fast picking up the smoothness and style of a pro. Belly dancing is her thing and she knows how to draw her audience right into her rhythmic movements. At the end of her show, the guys were shouting for more!

Completing the show at the Guys and Dolls are the lovely Brandy Wine and the very well known beauty **SILKI ST. JAMES.** Silki has just returned to Las Vegas from a successful theatre engagement in Los Angeles. "The Gourmet of the Runway," **ARTIE BROOKS** furnishes the laughter.

Bust lovers will get more than they can handle at the Cabaret in the person of **ANN MARIE** (pictured), 67-25-36. Her obvious assets are really drawing the crowds to the plush nightclub and she entertains the patrons royally with her singing, dancing, and comedy patter. Her theme song is "Thanks for the Mammaries!"

Also featured at the Cabaret is **TRACY SUMMERS** (pictured), whose face you cannot miss since it's the one staring down at you from billboards all over town. This sexy gal is definitely "Miss Personality." Tracy presents the audience with a variety of shows including a dynamite gypsy show, a "Wonder Woman" show, and now she's working on a space show.

There are five more sexy exotics on the same bill along with the outstanding comedy and magic of **PROFESSOR TURBAN**. You definitely get your

money's worth at the Cabaret.

A good friend of mine, **JUDY MICHAELS**, is performing for lucky patrons at the Jolly Trolley. Formerly the Centerfold, the club has been completely redecorated and features exotics and lovely go-go girls who not only dance for you but serve your drinks as well.

Vegas Visitor

February 16, 1977 A former Playboy Bunny in Chicago and a stewardess for TWA, you'll now find redheaded **TROUBLES GALORE** (pictured) entertaining lucky patrons at the Cabaret

Burlesque Palace.

Her start in burlesque came three years ago when she owned her own club back east. "My strippers just weren't showing up, so I went on myself!"

Troubles, who got her name from her husband, has spent most of her career in Ft. Lauderdale taking gigs for Cheetah II owner Bill Heywood who owns a string of clubs in the south. She and her husband raise Greyhound racing dogs on the side.

It was actually a movie that brought Troubles to Las Vegas. While performing at Cheetah III, a producer invited her to audition for a role in "Three Day Weekend," a comedy starring Roddy McDowell. She landed the role of Roddy's girl friend and had to go to Los Angeles for filming. While there, she met some people who knew **PAUL PERRY** and from that introduction came a two-week contract that has stretched into its eighth week and promises to continue indefinitely. "Three Day Weekend" is scheduled for release March 15.

Sometime later this spring Troubles is set for another role, this time as a mistress to the devil played by Cesar Romero in "Devil's Mistress." Troubles credits her experience on the burlesque stage with giving her the composure and stage presence necessary to land these plum parts. Look for her in the credits as Blake Parrish.

A Taurus, born on Friday the 13th, Troubles is 5'9" with measurements of 35-19-34. She puts her heart and soul in her huge variety of shows. Troubles incorporates a dazzling fire routine into most of her shows, which include a gangster routine, a country and western show, a rock show, a space show, and a cheerleader show.

"I like fast paced music with lots of dancing. I want to be thought of as an entertainer rather than just with lust. I move around so much that no one has time to say anything derogatory to me."

Troubles says she is mainly booked on the strength of her "Tribute to Elvis" show.

"I have an identical white cape and suit with over 5,000 rhinestones on it which was made for me in Acapulco. It took the seamstress three months to finish it. The show itself is 30 minutes long so I do it for special audiences."

One of her props in the show is a giant teddy bear. If you want to see what the teddy bear does you will just have to catch the show.

Troubles enjoys sculpting and choreographing other dancer's shows. She designs her wardrobe, most of which are made by **HEDY JO STAR**. She is also keeping a diary about her experiences as a stripper.

"I've already made arrangements to have it published. I figure on about two more years in burlesque. The story will probably be called *Diary of a Mad Stripper!* I've had a lot of insane things happen on the road."

P.S. Troubles is looking for a small poodle, preferably a teacup. If you need to give yours a good home, see Troubles at the Cabaret nightly.

Vegas Visitor

February 25, 1977   A master of disguise is **THE VELVET ODESSEY** (pictured) appearing at the Palomino Club. She is a redhead in "Sympathy for the Devil," a grey-haired old lady in the "Crazy Lady of Delta Dawn," a short, curly, black-haired moppet in "Betty Boop," and in the sensual "Future Fox," she dons a white Afro sprinkled with silver dust.

VELVET ODESSEY

"It is not so much a dance I do, as it is an erotic illusion. I create various scenarios," explains Velvet referring to a description of her unusual shows. "I like to act."

And act, she does. More than one patron has been heard to remark while watching the "Crazy Lady of Delta Dawn," "Listen to her laugh. It's maniacal. I don't think I'd like to be alone with her. She must be really crazy to laugh like that."

Then, in her next show, when she's wearing her white Afro and is decked out in layers of glittering rhinestone jewelry as the "Future Fox," Velvet proceeds to convince the same audience that she is a sexy lady who knows exactly what she is doing and wouldn't it be great if she'd do it with them – alone!

No matter who she is on stage, when she comes off from a show, she is uniquely herself, from her San Francisco dress of old time skirts, sweaters, shawls and boots to her apartment decorated in her words: "San Francisco funk and art nouveau," to her book case filled with literature on the metaphysics and the occult.

Adept at casting astrological charts, Velvet has done many charts for the dancers she works with, planning eventually to compare some of the aspects and see what, if anything, dancers have in common with each other.

Before coming to the burlesque circuit, Velvet was an executive secretary for a property management company in San Francisco for five years. After seeing a few exotic shows, she decided, "it looked like fun." She traded her

typewriter for a G-string and hit the road.

"I was a Navy brat and had already traveled all over the world and liked it so I guess it never got out of my blood. I still wanted to travel."

She was one half of the first love act team with Daiquiri St. John and toured the finest nightclubs in Japan and Hawaii. Upon her return to the states, Velvet began to solo and after a road engagement was booked into the Palomino where you can see her zany shows nightly.

Fans of **JAN FONTAINE** will find her starring Friday and Saturday nights at the Sun Dancer. She does three dynamite shows a night.

Look for an old time burlesque review opening soon at the Joker Club in North Las Vegas. Meantime you can still enjoy the casino and restaurant.

Thank you Forest Duke and Johnny Tillotson for making my television appearance such a pleasant experience on the Forest Duke Show.

Vegas Visitor

March 3, 1977 In response to an article about her in *Variety*, **GEORGETTE DANTE,** star of the "Rare 'N Bare" at the Royal Las Vegas, has just received a request from Theodore Fischer of *Oui Magazine* requesting a feature article and pictorial layout of this unique exotic performer.

Burlesque is often a family business as are many other forms of show business and this week Georgette Dante's mother **DELILAH DANTE** (pictured) can be seen performing at the Sundancer. Delilah is a beautiful, well-built lady with a 44" bust line and puts many a younger girl to shame and she

isn't afraid to admit to being 50 years old. And who says strippers have short careers?

Many exotics start their careers by entering the amateur nude dance contests held nightly at the Palomino Club. One of the young ladies who has won the contest several times is making her debut as a professional exotic in the daytime show at the Palomino. She's performing under the name of Terry Stone and brings to the stage the youth and enthusiasm of a beginner along with the grace, beauty, and ability to guarantee her an excellent and successful future as an exotic.

DELILAH DANTE

All of the girls at the Cabaret are gorgeous ladies and many of them have been featured in magazines such as *Playboy* and *Oui* and now **SNOWY SINCLAIR** (pictured) has been offered her THIRD contract with *Playboy*

Magazine. She has already appeared in the August '76 edition and is part of a book being released by *Playboy* called *The Fabulous Girls of Las Vegas*. She will be seen again in an upcoming edition of *Playboy*. Congratulations to a beautiful and photogenic miss!

SNOWY SINCLAIR

"Sassy Class" at the Sahara injects a bit of burlesque during one of their dance sequences when the chorus line does an imaginative strip on stage with the use of briefcases while they are changing costumes for the next routine!

Why, I wonder, did Denise Clemente, the talented vocalist, wear such a dull dress for her solo spot and then come out in a gorgeous white sequined gown for a two second finale? **SUZETTE SUMMERS**, the talented exotic in the mini-burlesque show at the Fremont Hotel, tells me there's been a few problems getting it all together but things are beginning to shape up. Any show Suzette performs in is a must-see. I also recommend Rona Boucher who not only does a sexy strip but is a talented vocalist as well.

Those of you who enjoy hilarious burlesque skits will love the new "Fevers Up" at the Landmark. Starring J. C. Curtiss, **BILL FANNING**, and Maggie Montgomery, and with some delightful choreography by Jerry Norman, you are sure to be thoroughly entertained.

Irving Benson, **CHARLIE VESPIA**, **DEXTER MAITLAND** (pictured) and his lovely daughter April Maitland raise gales of laughter nightly with their burlesque skits at the Holiday Casino in the "Wide World of Burlesque." I also enjoyed the magic of the amazing Ricco.

Yes, folks, burlesque thrives in Las Vegas and I'm proud to be part of it and for those of you who have asked, I appear nightly at the Palomino with my own brand of burlesque combining strip-tease and magic. Hope to see you there, too!

Vegas Visitor

March 1977 **SAMMY DAVIS JR.** (pictured) has to be one of the most congenial and generous celebrities to ever play Las Vegas. Last week, he hosted another of his famous show people and guests party at Caesars Palace to celebrate his opening in the play "Stop the World, I Want to Get Off" on Broadway in New York City. Sammy sent out personal invitations to all the show people to be his guests for dining and dancing 'til the wee hours.

One of the most endearing qualities about Sammy is that he is not a show business snob. I've often heard stars knock burlesque, snub their noses, and in some cases deny that is where they got their start, but Sammy loves everyone. He makes a special effort during each of his Las Vegas appearances to get out and see as many of the entertainers in all fields as he can.

The first time I met Sammy was my opening night at the Royal Las Vegas. He'd come in to say hi to **BOB MITCHELL**, one of his favorite comics, and to ask him to appear on his show Sammy and Company to play his horns. Bob plays THREE at a time!

After the show he came back stage to say hello to everyone and I was a bit embarrassed. I'd just finished dancing to "Mr. Bojangles" made so popular by Sammy, but the artist on my tape was Johnny Paycheck in keeping with my country western theme. Sammy just laughed.

He invited our cast to his show and although I am not normally an autograph hound (I'd like to be but sometimes I'm afraid to ask), I asked him to autograph my copy of *Yes, I Can,* a fantastic autobiography by Sammy, which I was reading in the dressing room. I explained the missing front cover, missing because I'd purchased it at a flea market in Florida for a quarter! Sammy laughed and signed it.

The next time I saw Sammy was at the Palomino Club and it was a most unbelievable coincidence. I was on stage dancing to Sammy's recording of "Candy Man" doing a bit of magic when in walked Sammy and some of his friends. Later he said he was as surprised as I was. He hadn't known he was even coming to the Palomino, just came on a last minute visit! I asked him how he felt about a stripper dancing to one of his songs. He said it was always thrilling to hear someone playing his recordings and he was honored.

At his recent bash at Caesars, in addition to the showgirls and dancers from all the big shows, and most of the stars on the Strip, there were a goodly number of waitresses and bartenders, the whole crew from the Maxim, as well as burlesque performers including **ANN MARIE, TRIANA ZZON,** Sunny Day, Lela Sherry**, JUDY MICHAELS, BOB MITCHEL, CHARLIE VESPIA,** and **TEDDY KING.**

Thank you Sammy for a wonderful evening and break a leg!

Note: Country singer **TEX MAR-SHAL** will be making a special guest appearance at the Longbranch Saloon, March 26.

Vegas Visitor April 1, 1977

The Picasso of X-rated films, **RUSS MEYERS** (pictured with Kitten Natividad) was in town recently, promoting his latest movie "Up" which is now playing at Cinemas I, II, and III. With 28 films grossing over 58 million dollars to his credit, Russ Meyers is an authority on what makes a sexy film.

"Unlike the hard-core pornography, we don't show penetration," he said, "and we have a story line, beautiful girls, a bit of humor, quality every step of the way."

Myers candidly admits, "I look for a big bust; the natural kind in a woman, and a strong square jaw in a man."

Many of the performers in Myers films are from the burlesque world.

MISS KITTEN NATIVIDAD "Miss Nude Universe," who is appearing at the Guys and Dolls, is one of the stars of the newly released "Up." She is also scheduled to perform in a forthcoming production. "She's a beautiful girl," says Mr. Meyers. "She's also an excellent mimic and actress."

Folk who remember **ANN MARIE**, (67 inch bust who packed the Cabaret in her recent engagement), can watch for her in a Russ Meyers film where she will play the part of a radio evangelist! One of the lines "lay your afflicted parts on the radio," will surely make many new Russ Meyers converts, I mean fans!

Asked whether he ever appears in any of his own films, Mr. Meyers replied, "only if absolutely necessary as in the part of a clerk. In front of the cameras is not my bag."

Actually he doesn't have time for it. Russ Meyers creates his own films from scratch including the story line, and then he is director, producer, promoter, and "janitor" and "referee!"

"Each film is my own baby," admits Mr. Meyers. His proudest achievement was the much-heralded and publicized "Beyond the Valley of the Dolls." It was also his biggest box office success.

CAMILLE 2000 (pictured) a long-legged (5'10") blonde amazon of a stripper is now being featured at the Guys and Dolls with choreography by Paul Markoff who's known for his work with Ann Corio, Tempest Storm, and Blaze Starr. Camille demonstrates her agility and grace in some of the most sensuous prop work in burlesque.

Camille has toured all over the USA, starting her exotic career in Miami Beach, Florida after winning the "Miss Anniston" beauty title in her home town of Anniston, Alabama as well as being the homecoming queen her senior year in high school.

Camille enjoys guitar, singing, and cooking and the excitement of a motorcycle ride, "I plan to eventually incorporate a motorcycle "Evil Knievel" style in my show."

With her height and build 38-26-37, Camille dreams of one day becoming a showgirl. "I've been learning all the necessary steps and I am just waiting for the chance to audition."

Also at the Guys and Dolls, is actress, dancer **ANGELIQUE PET-TYJOHN**, seen just last week as THE star of a Star Trek rerun.

Angelique has appeared in over 40 television series and about 30 films. She was also the lead nude dancer in Barry Ashton's "Vive Paree Vive."

Presently, Angelique is hard at work on an ESP act with the Great Tomsoni.

Special thanks go out to "Birds of the World" and **BOB MITCHELL** for the two beautiful ring-necked doves they gave me for my show.

I also want to express my gratitude to Le Ruse, a local magician for his suggestion of a dove production that I've incorporated in my show.

Vegas Visitor

April 8, 1977 She looks like a beautiful Aztec princess, royally clad in gowns of gold and rich brocades, yards of shimmering silks and satins, all laden with precious jewels, honoring the patrons of the Palomino by her very presence. **SALUMBA** (pictured), a spicy Cuban beauty, entertains her subjects with her sensuous, enticing routines much as the dancers of ancient times performed their rituals of dance for the Gods.

One of Salumba's most beautiful shows is a combination of belly dance movement (she was formerly a belly dancer) and the expert deft handling of two large pink ostrich feather fans bigger than she is. The routine with the fans is reminiscent of a Spanish flavored Sally Rand.

Salumba has some of the most elegant wardrobe in burlesque and she spends hours sewing, by hand, extra touches of richness to her costumes with more beads, rhinestones, and pearls.

Not content with the exercise she receives on stage during her shows, Salumba regularly works out at the gym and exercises even more in the dressing room. She also believes in health foods and vitamins. Her 36-23-35 body is proof positive that the extra care is worth it.

Away from work, Salumba spends two or more hours daily practicing at the piano and takes three lessons a week, eventually planning to be a piano teacher.

Salumba is also enrolled in a jazz class, wanting to add some more material to her shows. Never satisfied, she is always trying to better herself and is always looking for new steps, new routines, and even more elegant wardrobe for her shows. It is hard for me to see where she could improve!

Jay Orlando, the sax player in "Girls Ala Carte," at the Fremont is a show-stopper when he plays "Tuff" on the alto sax. I don't think there is any music sexier than the sax, and Jay certainly makes the most of it with his versatility on the sax, flute, and alto sax.

Pepper Davis, the comic, seems to have a bit of trouble in his warm-up routine but when he gets rolling, he's a very funny man. His soft shoe and tap dancing belie his 50 some odd years.

GEORGETTE DANTE, star of Rare 'N Bare at the Royal Las Vegas, has added another powerhouse show. She has an electric plate on which she stands and from it she can light torches with her bare hands as well as turn on light bulbs! Georgette plans to go on the road soon, so don't miss her show. You will never see another show like it anywhere.

THE VELVET ODESSEY is "Still Willin" as the "Queen of the Silver Dollar" in a new and most original country rock show performed nightly at the Palomino.

Guys and Dolls start their continuous burlesque lineup at about six in the morning and among the many lovely ladies is **DIEDRE RHODES**, former showgirl and former Miss Nude Photogenic. The lovely lass tells me that she is getting some new and more "elegant glad rags" for the stage. Diedre is one of those girls who would make a

potato sack look like the latest Paris fashion.

Making her Las Vegas debut is **HOLLAND STAR** (pictured) coming to us from Boston, Massachusetts. Holland, a tall blonde, blue-eyed beauty with measurements of 38-25-37 is a former private secretary as well as an advertising model for a top Boston photographer.

With a magnificent wardrobe by the famous **HEDY JO STARR,** Holland performs to a variety of music built around themes including the southern belle, the saloon girl, a "Hello Dolly" show and a space show. You can see her at the Palomino during the exciting daytime show, which gets underway at 2PM.

Vegas Visitor

April 15, 1977 Whether she's playing the part of a Parisian streetwalker, or hamming it up as the sultry Mae West, **CHRISTINE DARLING** (pictured) injects a bit of the untamed lioness into each of her exotic portrayals at the Palomino. With her blonde hair tumbling over her shoulders and her smoldering cat eyes, Christine evokes the very picture of sensual temptation.

She prefers her shows to tell a story. "I grew up watching every musical production show I could, and all the old numbers seemed to have a story behind them."

Christine was born and raised in New York City and unlike the public's conception of a "dumb blonde," Christine was an honor roll student who at one time pursued a career as a doctor but had to settle for being a dental assistant because she didn't have a flair for math.

She was also voted in her senior year as "most likely to be the editor of Life Magazine."

"Everyone thought I would become a literary genius! If they could see me now!"

Christine remembers well her first job as an exotic at the old 42nd St. Playhouse in New York City.

"I was with a date when he introduced me to a couple who were friends of his. The girl and I started talking which was a little difficult since she spoke almost no English and I didn't speak Spanish. Anyway she told me what fantastic money she made as a dancer and how I should try it.

I told her that I'd never had dance lessons or any kind of training and she said that was all right. I didn't need them. She finally convinced me to go to the theatre where she worked to talk to the manager. I didn't get the message that this was a burlesque theatre and when we got there and I saw all the signs advertising girls, girls, girls, and the word burlesque all across the front, I wanted to chicken out. I was curious though. I wanted to know more so I was introduced to Jacqueline George, the manager and she told me to come to work at seven. No audition, nothing, just come to work at seven. I explained I had no costumes and I didn't know what to do but she said she'd fix me up. My first night was really hilarious. I spent my time trying to hide my front from the audience, my back from the band that was playing behind me, and watching the wings where Jacqueline was dancing the show and I was imitating her movements."

After the initial fright, Christine quickly worked her way up to becoming one of the most sought after exotics in New York City and was recommended by **DEXTER MAITLAND** at the Follies to Ann Corio who, after seeing Christine, immediately signed her to a contract.

Four years ago, after touring the country with the Ann Corio Show, as well as starring in her own shows and in the Minksys, Christine came to Las Vegas to work for **PAUL PERRY** at the Palomino. Except for brief road bookings, Christine has made the Palomino home.

"I really enjoy working here. Burlesque is treated as a show and you're expected to be good. You get the best lights, stage and sound. You get respect. If I had to go on the road again, I think I'd retire."

Vegas Visitor

April 22, 1977 **MARCELLA** (pictured) is just one of the unbelievably beautiful Misters at the Carrousel De Paris, appearing nightly in an exciting transsexual burlesque review. Direct from France, the show is a mixture of French naughtiness, sophisticated humor and the mysteries of "is she a he . . . or?"

MARCELLA
CARROUSEL DE PARIS

The Misters Akiko, Marcella, Danielle, Chouchou, and Mona Trieste, draw many an envious gaze from women because they are not only in fantastic shape but they all seem to have walked out of Vogue Magazine, capturing the high cheekbones and svelte sophistication of a Paris model and the grace and sensuality of the most erotic exotic. The show begins with a typical strip by

Chouchou who incorporates a bit of audience participation as she sings her desire for a King Kong and checks the male members of the audience for a hairy chest. Then Mona, as King Kong, enters the stage and after some sensual teasing, Chouchou unveils King Kong as Mona and they go into a sisterly-brotherly act or brotherly-sisterly act, depending on your point of view.

Camille, owner of Las Vegas' newest nightspot, has plans to bring more acts in from her native France in the next few months. She also invites patrons to enjoy the disco dancing between the three entirely different shows offered each night.

Two-time winner of the Lounge Comedy Star of the Year Award, Rip Taylor, is currently doing SRO at the Sahara Casbar and puts on one of the fastest paced, most entertaining comedy shows in town. It is easy to see why Rip has become such a sought after personality. In addition to his frequent appearances at the Sahara in the Casbar and in the Sahara as co-headliner with some of the country's biggest stars, Rip is also

appearing in several television shows. Last week he was on the Gong show panel and this week on The Brady Family.

His trade marks of the garbage can full of visual aids and his outlandish cape resembling a silver Christmas tree, help prepare the audience for his hilarious, fast-paced comedy. He tells more jokes in five minutes than you hear all year on some of the television comedy shows.

Rip's impersonation of Louis Armstrong, complete with toy horn for the visual effect, is a showstopper. Not only is the voice right on but he also brings many of the famous Armstrong facial movements into his impersonation.

Rip uses his vocal talents well, weaving song lines in and out of his comedy patter and closes his show appropriately with "You Made Me Love You, I Didn't Want to Do It" and the whole audience agrees. I found myself, clutching my prize of one of Rip Taylor's autographed pictures, with one of those idiotic smiles on my face and just a bit more lift in my step.

Vegas Visitor

April 29, 1977   After a successful and much talked about 30-week engagement at the Cabaret, **TURBAN** leaves Las Vegas for tropical Guam. Language is no barrier for this talented performer who has mastered the art of pantomime, which he combines with his magic to thoroughly captivate any audience and overcome any communication problems. Magic is a universal art

and is appreciated and applauded everywhere. Bon voyage, Turban.

One of the busiest exotics in town is **JAN FONTAINE** (pictured) who is presently appearing in the daytime show at the Palomino and in the nighttime show at the Sundancer. Spare time is devoted to her hobbies of flying and motorcycle riding.

JAN FONTAINE

Back after a short vacation in California is **GEORGETTE DANTE**, star of "Rare 'n Bare" at the Royal Las Vegas. She is set to appear in a movie about Jack Ruby.

Tiffany Holiday is now doing the emcee honors for the Cabaret. Tiffany is a very funny comedienne using a sexy Mae West voice and delivery as she tickles your funny bone.

SATAN'S ANGEL is preparing to open her own pet-grooming salon. Satan has appeared in Las Vegas several times, most recently at the Palomino.

The star of "Tickle My Fancy" at the Silverbird, Craig Russell, is a talented female impersonator and does a funny version of Carol Channing as well as Barbra Streisand and Totie Fields. The highly successful play is a production of Entertainment Properties Inc. headed by Joseph Donato and is expected to run indefinitely.

LIZA JOURDAN, a beautiful blonde exotic at the Cabaret, can count on the very best lighting because her mother, once a top exotic working under the name of Caprice, is now in charge of the lights and sound!

Be sure and catch "Girls Ala Carte" at the Fremont Hotel starring exotic **SUZETTE SUMMERS**. The last word is that the show may close May 8 but then it may move to another showroom.

My thanks go to Forest Duke and Bert Convy for making my appearance on the Forest Duke Show such a pleasure.

Vegas Visitor

May 13, 1977 Rarely can an exotic make so much claim to fame in six months as Penthouse cover girl **VA-LERIE RAY** (pictured) appearing now at the Cabaret.

With the help of George Fullwood, her costume designer and choreographer, Valerie is showing that with planning and hard work, a girl can go as far as she wants and not have to hope for a lucky break. Valerie has been making her own luck.

She posed for the Penthouse layout over a year before it was published. She made the rounds of movie producers and secured good parts in "Skateboard" and Gore Vidal's "Caligula."

Then, she secured the aid of George Fullwood in putting together her first exotic show which she debuted at the Other Ball, a plush nightspot in San Gabriel, California.

Her first Las Vegas appearance was deliberately timed for the release of the May issue of Penthouse which features Valerie not only as the cover girl but also in a most revealing centerfold layout.

She is in the process of negotiating for further film deals as well as several exciting road offers.

ANGELIQUE PETTYJOHN actress, singer, and exotic is being held over by popular demand at Guys and Dolls. Angelique uses all of her assets and talents in a performance guaranteed to raise your temperature.

Beautiful Genieve, third runner-up to the Miss Nude America pageant, is making her Las Vegas debut at the Palomino, giving new life to a selection of show tunes including "Cabaret," "If You Could See Me Now," and "You Gotta Have A Gimmick."

Bosom lovers will adore **JODY ENGLISH** (pictured). Working relief at the Palomino on the day shift, Jody fills her nights managing the Sundancer.

Lovey Goldmine credits George Fullwood with the choreography in her entertaining "Champagne Taste" number. This redheaded beauty is a talented pantomimist and creative dancer and comes to the Cabaret after a long engagement at the Crazy Horse Saloon in Paris.

Hope you enjoyed the **DICK MAURICE SHOW** (pictured) on Channel 5 Sunday. I'd like to thank his guests including **SUZETTE SUM-MERS, CASSANDRA LEE,** and **GEORGETTE DANTE**, for making the interview so interesting. My thanks go to Dick Maurice and Jess Mack who made it possible.

LAS VEGAS PANORAMA—25

STRIPPERS — Controversial, provocative and definitely informative Strippers, Georgette Dante, Suzette Sommers, Casandra Lee and Dusty Sommers [l to r] let it all hang out on Dick Maurice & Company Sunday night at 10 p.m. on TV-5.

Vegas Visitor

May 20, 1977 The first time international burlesque agent **JESS MACK** came to Las Vegas was in 1944 when he worked as straight man for Charlie Kemper at the El Rancho Vegas.

"There were only two clubs on the Strip then," relates Jess, "the El Rancho Vegas and the Frontier. There wasn't any big freeway, just a two-lane road called the LA Highway and I rode horseback through Caesars Palace. I loved Las Vegas. Then, Helldorado was REAL. I vowed then, I'd be back!"

In the between time, Jess continued to be the straight man in shows like **"GEORGE WHITE'S SCANDALS"** (pictured). He wrote material for the comic greats in burlesque including Jackie Gleason, Phil Silvers, and Abbott and Costello. Jess worked in every possible capacity in show business including producing and directing.

Jess worked with the tops in the entertainment field and they all counted on him for that extra gag. Gleason and Silvers credit Jess with much of their later movie success. He also published burlesque's classiest publication, *Cavalcade of Burlesque.*

38

Jess met his wife Dorothy (pictured) 25 years ago when they worked in the same show. Dorothy was singing and dancing in a sister act. But they were both married and did not come together until both were widowed. Dorothy and Jess were married in 1968 in Las Vegas and returned to New York City where Jess had moved his agency business from Boston after his first wife's death. Dorothy was working for ABC as a costume designer, collaborating with such designers as Bob Mackie on wardrobe for shows including "Let's Make a Deal," "Dating Game," "Lawrence Welk,"and a host of daytime soap operas.

Jess says about that time he was giving thoughts to relocating and slowing down, so he and his lovely bride moved to Las Vegas in 1971.

"Yes, he moved here just like he's always wanted to," says Dorothy, "but he didn't slow down!"

Jess admits to hours as late as midnight most nights and often a seven-day week. A member of every conceivable organization, Jess is especially fond of those that support charitable goals.

Among the list of myriad accomplishments is having been selected by the Screen Actors Guild as a franchised agent. Last year he was made an honorary mayor of Atlantic City, which should be of value in the future when Atlantic City follows the neon footsteps of glamorous Las Vegas.

Dorothy and Jess (pictured as they are today) take great pride in their only son Richard. Writing under the pseudonym Richard Saunders, he has just had his first book *Collecting and Restoring Wicker Furniture* published by Crown Publishers.

For Dorothy and Jess, their agency is not only their job, it's their hobby as well. They love to show visitors their extensive collection of photos and Jess boasts of the largest collection of burlesque scenes and gags in the business.

If you need a booking, want to learn some gags, want to buy a whole show or just one of the best acts in burlesque including Georgina Spellman ("Devil in Miss Jones"), Georgette Dante, Busty Russell, and Jennifer Fox, contact the Jess Mack Agency.

Vegas Visitor

May 1977 From secretary to stripper, Brandi Britan is a sample of the sweets offered at the world famous totally nude Palomino Club in North Las Vegas.

Brandi has only been in the exotic business five months but is already developing that important desire to please an audience and judging from the response of her audience, doing it very well.

Says Brandi: "Onstage I try to come on as the girl next door. I try to have as much eye contact as possible with the people. I want each guy to feel I'm dancing for him! I feel very sexy when I do floor work on the runway, very close to my audience. It's to please them and not just because it is a job. I really like my work."

Brandi looks like the mischievous little girl next door with blonde hair, lively brown eyes and her petite measurements of 33-22-34 on a 5'3", 116 lb. frame.

Her show is anything but little girl as

she teases and pleases complete with nylon and garter belt and a "come and get it" expression that makes it hard for the guys to stay in their seats.

Brandi has an extensive background in dance with eight years of ballet and four years of jazz. She enjoys the challenge of making up sexy new routines.

Although she plans to continue dancing for a long time, Brandi would eventually like to finish college and have her own school where she will teach retarded children.

Meanwhile she's teaching some pretty interesting lessons in the daytime show at the Palomino.

Vegas Visitor

May 27, 1977 Hazel-eyed and blonde 38-22-36 **LIZA JOURDAN** (pictured), "the girl with the bedroom eyes," beckons you into her boudoir for the most sensuous carnation-scented bubble bath in burlesque. JoAnn, her mother, watches each move from the light booth as she chooses the most flattering light patterns for her daughter!

The highly unusual combination of mother and daughter in burlesque is at the Cabaret Burlesque Palace. However, in their case it is a logical arrangement because JoAnn was once an exotic herself under the name of Caprice.

Liza says that her mother did not encourage her in her pursuit of burlesque because she wanted her to finish school. Liza had been attending Valley College in San Fernando majoring in law research. She dropped out of college temporarily to take a six-week engagement at the Cabaret which has extended itself into a six-month gig so far. "I haven't given up school," says Liza positively, "I expect to return soon but in the meantime this job is the best living a girl can make. I really enjoy it and it pays for my tuition."

When asked who taught Liza how to strip, both mother and daughter sort of shrug their shoulders. "Actually I had the benefit of seeing lots of exotics before I tried it and I even caught my mother's wardrobe at the Follies in Los Angeles. When I decided to dance, I used my mother's agent, got myself some wardrobe which mother helped me with and bluffed my way through the first performance."

"She just picked it up, the same as I did," says JoAnn very proudly. "And I think she's done a good job."

JoAnn (Caprice) was one of the first exotic dancers to perform on the Las Vegas Strip at the Silver Slipper in a Barry Ashton review. "I'd been in the chorus line six months and they needed an exotic. They were desperate and on the basis of some experience I'd picked up in San Diego, I was it."

Being "it" also meant that JoAnn did a lot of the scenes with burlesque greats including Irving Benson, Hank Henry, **DEXTER MAITLAND**, and Lenny Bruce.

Asked how she feels about stripping today, JoAnn says, "I think it's great! It's more honest. Who doesn't know what's under a pastie or a two-inch piece of material. We're all alike and I think the body is a work of art. Maybe that's why all the great artists paint nudes. I enjoy watching strippers perform, which is an art itself."

Liza got her experience in burlesque just as her mother did, "trial and error." Before coming to the Cabaret, she was a featured exotic at the Body Shop and the Pink Pussy Cat in Los Angeles.

When not performing, Liza spends a lot of time on the tennis courts, keeping her enviable figure in shape. She also enjoys a wide variety of reading material including most of the women's magazines.

Rehearsals are in progress now for an old time burlesque review to open at the Joker. Set to open at the North Las Vegas nightspot are **BOB MITCHELL, CHARLIE VESPIA** and **CHRISTINE DARLING**. The rest of the cast is, as yet, unannounced.

Vegas Visitor

June 10, 1977 One of Las Vegas' most popular comics is **BOB MITCHELL** (pictured), star of "Jokers Wild Burlesque" in North Las Vegas. Known for his story-telling abilities and his ability to play two or three horns at a time, Bob is also a top character actor as is demonstrated nightly in this show's classic burlesque scenes.

Bob started his career at 13 years old at the Colony Club in Louisville, Kentucky where he worked in the band. He had to have a special work permit to play his horns there and between shows he wasn't allowed in the club.

A self-taught musician, Bob toured all over the country appearing with Claude Thornhill's Band in the big band era and forming his own group, The Untouchables. "We were the first band to swing by our heels from a trapeze while we played our horns. That was three years before the Goofers did it on television. After they did it, we quit because all of a sudden we were the copycats."

One night when the regular emcee was involved in an auto accident, Bob stepped forward to assume the role of emcee. He was such a hit that a local agent suggested he continue as emcee and immediately booked him into an East St. Louis, Illinois nightspot called Jimmy's Gay Inn (it wasn't). There, St. Louis agent Mike Raft spotted the promising young entertainer and booked him into the Theatre Lounge in Dallas, Texas owned by Bernie Wienstein.

"He was a great guy to work for," says Bob. "He had a plaque up over the door that said: 'My customers are NOT always right. My entertainers are.' If he thought a customer was getting out of line, he'd go up and ask him how much money he figured he'd spent. Then he'd take the money out of his pocket, give it to the guy and tell him never to come back."

It was in Dallas that Bob worked with stripper Candy Barr and also co-starred with her in an X-rated movie called "Smart Alec." "Everything was simulated, but "Smart Alec" was the biggest grossing X-rated movie until "Deep Throat," said Bob.

As a musician, Bob won the Ted Mack Original Amateur Hour three times. He also won the amateur of the year finals and that got him a spot on the Johnny Carson Show. "Unfortunately, at that time, the first 15 minutes of Johnny's show was only shown locally in New York City and that was the segment I appeared on with Skitch Henderson."

Recently, Bob was a guest of **SAMMY DAVIS JR.** on his show Sammy and Company.

Bob has been appearing in Las Vegas since 1966 starring in shows at Caesar's Palace, Fremont Hotel, Circus Circus, and the Royal Las Vegas. He got his start in Las Vegas at the old Gay Nineties for nightclub mogul **PAUL PERRY**. He has also worked for Paul at the Cabaret, the Palomino and now the Joker Club.

In his spare time Bob loves to write stories and songs. He'd like someday to become a producer.

"My real ambition is to open a home where I can raise about 25 or 30 children. I love children. I have five of my own."

Bob also has quite a reputation as a cook, finding most any excuse to give an impromptu dinner party for 15 or 20 "drop-in" guests. And when there's anything left over, he brings it to the club and feeds everyone there.

Known for his generosity, Bob is always putting someone up for a few days or a few months. His helping hand is always out, making it clear that he doesn't expect anything in return. He genuinely likes to help others.

Bob belongs to several charitable organizations and is on the board of directors for Saints and Sinners as well as acting as one of their Jesters. He is secretary of the Las Vegas chapter of Kentucky Colonels.

Wednesday nights always finds Bob at the boxing matches and after matches he is a terror on the slot machines!

Vegas Visitor

June 17, 1977 One of the most prominent show business couples in Las Vegas is **JIM "VEGAS VAMPIRE" PARKER** and his lovely wife, former exotic star now burlesque columnist, **P.J. PARKER** (pictured).

P.J., who performed as an acrobatic exotic for **PAUL PERRY** at the Palomino and the Cabaret, had to retire after slipping on a feather during her performance which left her with a knee injury.

A member of a burlesque family which includes sister: exotic **AMBER MIST**, mother Ava Leigh and father, comic Gene Graham, P.J. toured the country in a carnival show during summer vacation from a Catholic boarding school she and her sister attended 14 years. "I wavered between wanting to be a nun and wanting to be a stripper. I chose stripper because I wanted to have children."

P.J. relates that her first performance came at the age of 13. "The regular girls in the show had demanded a raise my mother couldn't afford and so they all quit. There was only the family left. I started out in a leotard and went down to full pants, net bra and pasties."

She first stripped under the name of Velvet Knight because she had dark hair. To make her look older, the girls in the show bleached her hair with a combination of peroxide, ammonia, and Lux Dishwashing Liquid. From that unlikely mixture was born a blonde exotic, Paulette Powers.

Her show changed too. Flashier costumes and a unique opening from a beautiful oyster shell combined with her superb agility and grace as a dancer made her a much sought after exotic.

"The oyster shell was a beautiful opening," says Paulette, "but I remember a funny incident on stage with the shell. The opening and closing were controlled backstage and one night as I got back in the shell and it started to close, I saw this dog I'd been friendly with coming on stage, howling and barking. It almost got its head caught in the shell trying to rescue me!"

Jim also worked in burlesque. "I was a comic in the carnival circuit. Before I went in the service I was part of a comedy act that was a takeoff on wrestling. I was the referee."

Back from the service, Jim worked as a stand-up comic in burlesque mostly around Milwaukee where he also attended the University of Wisconsin.

"From there I drifted into radio as a dee jay. The story of my first job is a comedy scene itself," Jim relates. "I'd already made a lot of those interviews with the usual don't call me, I'll call you results. One day as I was about to get the same story the police came in and arrested the man at the control board who'd been caught flashing at the playground. This created a vacancy and my first job as a dee jay!"

With the benefit of a good education and his natural ability at comedy and writing, Jim began to create his own press releases and other radio material.

When he came to Las Vegas he worked as a columnist for the Sun Scene Magazine and was news director for KORK and KLUC-TV.

Jim also made cinema history when he starred in the first horror-porno film "Hot Vampires." "The film's lead was just a character part. They wouldn't let me do any of the athletic scenes. Maybe they figured I couldn't stand up under the pressure?"

He also played a detective in "Trip With The Teacher" and a mafia hit man in "Massacre Mafia Style."

The Parker's plans for the future include possible production work in television and movies. As P.J. says, "We're not pushing for anything, we're just taking things as they come."

The Parkers will be celebrating their third wedding anniversary July 28.

Although they have no children yet, "we're working on it," they do have their hands full raising seven Chihuahuas.

Herbie Fay, best known for his role as Corporal Fender on Phil Silvers, "Sgt. Bilko" is recuperating from a broken hip at West Charleston Convalescent home. Cheer him up by dropping him a line or visiting him. Doctors say it will be a month or two before the 77-year-old comic is up and about. His most recent role was as Ben Golman in "Doc."

Tiffany Holiday, Cabaret comedienne, was injured in an auto accident and will be off work for a while. All of her many friends wish her a speedy recover.

TURBAN, comic-magician, is now host and emcee for the world famous amateur nude dance contest at the Palomino.

Vegas Visitor

June 24, 1977 "While she was making me eat fire, she picked the watch right off my wrist. I didn't even know it was gone!"

"She had me stand on her stomach while she was doing a back bend and if that wasn't enough, my brother was standing there with me."

"She said she'd flick the cigarette tip out of my hand. I was shaking when I held it out. She flicked the tip twice and sent sparks everywhere and there was still almost a whole cigarette left for me to smoke."

"Yeah, when she made me eat the fire, she picked my inside coat pocket of a cigar which she put in my mouth and then she lit it with the fire she blew from her own mouth!"

Unbelievable? Yes, but true. These are some of the after-show comments on our bionic exotic **GEORGETTE DANTE** (pictured), star of the Royal Las Vegas "Rare 'N Bare" show.

Georgette treats her audience to a wide variety of her skills which include fire dancer, acrobatic dancer, bull whip artist, weight lifting artist, and pick pocket expert. She undoubtedly has the fastest paced most unusual show in burlesque. When she shakes to "Wipe Out," she's resting!

I've had the privilege of knowing and working with Georgette several times and I think her most remarkable feat is the successful diet that trimmed some 50 pounds off her body to give her a slender trim figure and a new image.

This photo, taken at Surfside 7 in Ft. Walton Beach, Florida three years ago, shows Georgette posing in the lobby with **TURBAN** (now appearing at the Palomino) and me on each shoulder. She weighed about 175 pounds at the time!

Now a svelte 125 lbs., Georgette has trimmed away excess weight but she still maintains her incredible strength and is even more amazing as she tosses 200 lb. men around the stage and lifts 50 pound chairs up in the air with one hand while she's twirling tassels. Yes, this girl wastes no effort and doesn't have to look for things to do to "kill" time.

Georgette has been in show business since she was five years old and her parents dressed her as a midget for the carnival. She's been in burlesque since she was 12 years old and has appeared in all the top nightspots in the country.

For the kind of show that chills you to the bone in much the same way as the high flyers in a trapeze show, with a touch of humor throughout and more than enough to talk about for days, be sure and catch Georgette Dante at the Royal Las Vegas.

Vegas Visitor

July 1, 1977 There's nobody quite like **BOB MITCHELL** and **CHARLIE VESPIA** (pictured) when the two of them team up for old time burlesque scenes at the Joker Club in North Las Vegas.

Giving the old classics like *the crazy house* and *the movie scene* new life with their hilarious characterizations, and adding riotous, ad-libs as they go, Bob and Charlie keep the audience in stitches. There hasn't been as well matched a comedy team since Abbott and Costello.

Also featured is Las Vegas sexiest exotic dancer **SUZETTE SUMMERS**. A strip teaser in the most literal sense, Suzette combines the charms of Delilah with the movements of a Swiss time-piece weaving a magic spell of sexual fantasy for everyone.

CHRISTINE DARLING presents her own tribute to Mae West and has all the figure and personality to convince. She is also dynamite as the straight lady in the burlesque scenes.

Also featured is "Miss Perpetual Motion," **JAN FONTAINE** who never stops moving from the moment she steps on stage until her breathless exit ten minutes later.

The final member of the "Jokers Wild Burlesque" revue is yours truly. I present the "only wild west magic show in burlesque" as well as "a touch of magic" in another one of my shows.

Now in her second week at the Caba-ret is **DI ALBA**. From Miami Beach, Florida, this Cuban beauty looks just like she stepped out of Star Trek.

GINA BON BON, "The Love Po-tion Candy Girl," has just opened at Guys and Dolls.

Vivacious redhead **JUDY MICHAELS** is now starring in her own show at the Crazy Horse. Backed by a seven-piece band called Total Unity, Judy performs a unique acrobatic exotic show. Judy will also be acting as assistant to David Lean at Channel 5 in commercial productions.

For a real treat, drop into the Jolly Trolley for a steak dinner and a peak at the "Centerfold Revue."

Vegas Visitor

July 1977 The new "Wild World of Burlesque" revue at the Holiday Casino generates enough energy throughout the fun-packed show to keep its patrons smiling for hours after the last seat is emptied.

The Holiday Dancers, choreographed by Betty Francisco, move through their dance routines with perfect timing, smiling, twirling, jumping, leaping, shaking, and that's just in the first eight counts! Plenty of imaginative credit belongs to Betty Francisco for a show that displays originality and creativity and something else few chorus line routines achieve: sexiness!

The Amazing Rico is fun to watch as he cavorts with a member of the audience through the popular cut and restored rope routine. His facial expressions as he performs the silks and appearing and multiplying candles are priceless. He leaves no doubt that he is confident of his skill and you should be too. The popular zigzag illusion gave the audience the chance to view one of the most baffling magical effects in history. I'd seen it on television many times and Rico presents the astounding feat with great style.

Featured belly dancer in the show is Sumi. Although a very beautiful girl, she is not one of the most talented belly dancers I've seen; or maybe it was an off night?

The real highlight of the show is without a doubt, the hilarious Snyder Brothers. Kenny Snyder makes an instant smash with the audience as he gives a cooking lesson, sampling an assortment of liquors as he adds them to his recipe. He gets tipsier and tipsier until his final "check-em out" which is a taste of prune juice sent by Anita Bryant after which he remarks that it's time to "run."

Is there anything these talented brothers can't do? From the vocal impressions of singing greats like Dean Martin, Glen Campbell, and Tony Bennett by Bobby with the back-up comedy illustrations of Kenny, the Snyder's are wonderful!

GEORGETTE DANTE closed at the Royal Las Vegas and will appear in the Ann Corio Broadway production "This Was Burlesque." The long-running production makes its first appearance of this season in Lathan, New York following Ann-Margret.

Georgette credits stories such as those in *Variety, Oui Magazine, Panorama,* and *Vegas Visitor* for bringing her to the attention of Ann Corio.

The new feature taking Georgette's spot is our own *Vegas Visitor* columnist **SUZANNE VEGAS** with her singing, dancing, and comedy talents on display in an act called "A Tribute to Las Vegas." This highly popular and well-known exotic has been a big draw to many nightspots in Las Vegas and makes a winning addition to Rare 'N Bare.

From New York comes **AMARET-TA**, a lovely brunette, performing nightly at the world-famous Palomino.

And don't forget, for old time burlesque, it's "Jokers Wild Burlesque" located across the street from the Palomino in North Las Vegas.

Vegas Visitor

July 8, 1977 Bubbling with little-girl enthusiasm, **SUZANNE VEGAS** (pictured) transforms the stage of the Royal Las Vegas into a show business tribute to Las Vegas as she sings, dances, and talks her way through a highly polished performance.

Anything but a little girl, Suzanne a 36-23-35, red headed beauty, has been in the entertainment field since she was a year and a half. She appeared on Broadway at age 15 in "Stop The World, I Want to Get Off." Her resume reads like a who's who sheet and includes several motion pictures. She co-starred in "Pageant" with John Barrymore, Jr.. Suzanne has appeared on every local television and radio show as well as several national shows. She's a beauty title winner, capturing the "Miss Film World," "Miss Democrat" and "Miss

Beautiful Legs" titles.

Suzanne has appeared with over 30 internationally known stars including Norm Crosby most recently at the Hyatt Regency in Los Angeles. She's also guested with Connie Stevens, Jerry Lewis, Rip Taylor, Don Ho, Olivia Newton-John, and that's just a ripple in the list.

Suzanne has been the lead dancer in many strip production shows as well as the star of her own revue. And when she's not busy in Las Vegas, she tours the country with her highly versatile act appearing in such gems as the Hollywood Palladium, Coconut Grove/Ambassador, and the Regency Hyatt House as well as some of the more familiar burlesque nightclubs such as Skulls Rainbow Room in Nashville and the Follies Theatre in New York City.

SUZANNE VEGAS

Wherever she's appearing, Suzanne writes. Presently a columnist in our own Vegas Visitor, she also guest writes for the newspapers in whatever town she's appearing in.

Her column "Backstage" represents every facet of show business. The personalities who appear in her stories range from the immediately recognizable names of Sammy Davis Jr., Juliet Prowse, Joey Bishop, and Monty Hall, to the third girl in the fourth row of the biggest production shows on the strip.

Her performance as star of "Rare 'N Bare" gives her the chance to demonstrate her talents as she sings "Viva Las Vegas" in a style reminiscent of Ann Margret, soft and sexy, and dances her way through selections like Ronnie Laws, "Fever." She gives the audience a glimpse of her background when she tells them, "I decided to come to Las Vegas when I was 17 and my mother was horrified. All that drinking and gambling and all those nude women? My father wanted to come along!"

As she goes into her final number, gracefully manipulating two huge fans a la Sally Rand, undulating on a circular prop, utilizing the whole stage in a series of perfectly timed kicks and splits, and climaxing in a perfectly posed split on the prop, it's apparent she has won everyone's heart and delivered a memorable evening of entertainment.

Vegas Visitor

July 15, 1977 "If you could dance, you weren't a stripper!" so relates **JONI JANSEN** (pictured), now appearing at the Jolly Trolley, as we discussed her career which started at the Jungle Lounge in Louisville, Kentucky.

Joni started out as a go-go dancer in a cage working for $2.60 an hour (ten cents more an hour than I made in Phoenix!). "They told me I was just wasting my time and that I should try stripping for which they paid me a whole $75 a week. I watched the other girls – old time strippers – not dancers at all. They were graceful walkers. I picked up a bit here and there and **BOB MITCH-ELL** helped me a lot, giving me ideas for an act."

That act is best associated with a sexy, skin-tight red dress, lots of black ostrich marabou, a big red hat also trimmed in marabou and ostrich plumes, and an opening to "Mame." After seductively peeling off most of her wardrobe, Joni goes into some graceful contortions on a revolving circular prop. One of the remarks I've heard during her performance is "She's a lady." And that she is; a very sexy lady.

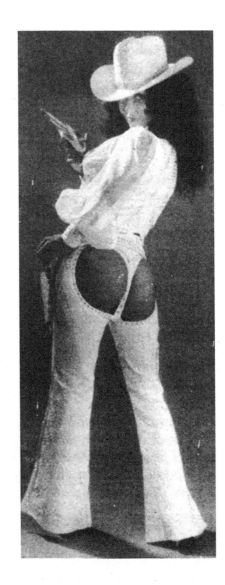

Besides her present appearance at the Jolly Trolley, Joni has also been featured in "Burlesk Burlesk" at Circus Circus, "Burlesk '76" at the Royal Las Vegas, and the old Gay Nineties.

Sharing the spotlight with Joni at the Jolly Trolley are tall, graceful redheaded, Chris Cockneuer, De De Diamond, and Favor O'Day.

JAN FONTAINE, who appears at the Joker Club, has several interesting hobbies. She is a licensed pilot and thinks nothing of rising early in the morning to fly to places like Lake Havasu for lunch or to Blythe for a spot of tea. When she's home, she says that rafting is her favorite past time.

SUSI MIDNIGHT and **VELVET ODESSEY**, two of the Palomino exotics, were discussing the jewels Susi flashes on her fingers. Says Susi, "I've never taken any of them off. I guess that shows how much I love them." "No," says Velvet, "It just shows you've never been hungry!"

Vegas Visitor

July 22, 1977 If you like the unusual in burlesque, you'll certainly find it at the Silver Slipper in "This is Boy-Lesque." I took my 74-year-old grandmother to see the show starring female impersonator **KENNY KERR** (pictured). Grandma nudged me all through the show with the question "now this one is a girl, right?"

No Grandma, they're all men with the clothes, the carriage, the bearing and the mannerisms of the greatest female stars in the world. You've just seen a marvelous Barbra Streisand aka Kenny Kerr, an almost more real than the real Carol Channing aka Jan North, and the exciting Diana Ross aka Artie Jones.

You've also caught a glimpse of Marlene Dietrich, Shirley Bassey, Cher, Tina Turner, and other famous stars.

The only strip in the show is Kenny Kerr's Queen of the Strippers, which included a fire show. On this night, he added a bit more drama when he almost lost his G-string!

Comedy is provided in Bobby Baines pantomime of the drunken version of "Twelve Days of Christmas" and Al Munson and Kenny Kerr aka "Her Royal Highness the Princess of Monrovia" (a Carol Burnett skit) – hilarious.

Backstage, Kenny introduced me to his mother who flew in for Kenny's opening. His family is proud of his career and more family members plan to catch his show at the Slipper.

Costume designer, **HEDY JO STAR,** created most of Kenny's wardrobe. "She's fantastic," says Kenny. Kenny also makes some of his own gowns including the one he wears as Streisand.

Future plans for Kenny include a possible television pilot, "a situation comedy show," explains "Boy-Lesque" producer Dr. Jack.

The show is expected to run indefinitely and includes Terry Daniels, Roger Caldwell, and Mickey St. Michaels.

Vegas Visitor

July 1977 One of the classiest exotics in town, **GYPSY LOUISE** 38-25-36 (pictured), is now appearing at the Palomino Club in North Las Vegas.

Originally from Los Angeles where she worked as a beautician, beauty school instructor, and pool hustler, Gypsy has been appearing at the Cabaret, Joker Club, and Palomino over the last several years.

She describes her own act as "sensuous." And it is that, but it is also much more. Gypsy combines her impish sense of humor, lots of graceful movement in filmy negligees, and selections in music from country to Tom Jones to give an intriguing glimpse of a pleasing personality.

She admits that she would really like to be a comedienne like her favorites Carol Burnett and Lucille Ball. She also enjoys Redd Foxx and Don Rickles.

"I like to kid around with the audience and make them feel more comfortable," explains Gypsy, " and a good sense of humor seems to help."

Gypsy who is 5' 8'" tall used to be a model for Butterick, Simplicity and McCall's patterns. She's also done a few commercials including Hires Root Beer.

In her spare time, Gypsy practices shooting with her .22 and .38 revolvers. She is an excellent marksman.

One of her many hobbies is disco dancing. She particularly favors the Brewery and Jubilation discos. Gypsy also enjoys sewing, cooking, eating out and men with lots of money!

Vegas Visitor

August 5, 1977 The world of opera lost a great talent when Barry Ashton signed **CHARLIE VESPIA** (pictured) in 1967 for his burlesque show at the Riverside in Reno.

Now appearing at the Joker Club in North Las Vegas with **BOB MITCHELL** in "Jokers Wild Burlesque," Charlie has become one of the Las Vegas' best known and loved straight men. Fondly called "the peanut man" in recognition of his original interpretation of the famous candy butcher routine, Charlie astounds audiences with his hilarious entrance and caps it with an a cappella rendition of "Arrivederci Roma" or "O Sole Mio."

Charlie explains the origination of his peanut vendor routine: "Barry Ashton suggested I do the bit up front of the show. He said, "Why don't you go out and sell some peanuts?" I thought he was nuts but I tried it. Each time, I added something new based on the audiences reactions."

When Charlie first joined Barry Ashton's show, he was part of a duet performing as a comedy-singing team with his brother. Later, Barry and his partner Wolf cast Charlie in several burlesque bits, the first one being as the faggot in the "Transformer" scene.

"I was arbitrarily picked from the cast to be the faggot," says Charlie. "I was so green that first time. I didn't know anything about what I was doing. I just went out and pretended I WAS a faggot."

Charlie's faggot is so good, it is

almost embarrassing to Charlie who is married and the father of SEVEN children. "After a show, some customer will ask me if I AM and even though I show them the pictures of my family, I can still hear them say as I walk away, "But he has to be. No one straight could play it that good."

Charlie's formula for success explains his believability. "Anything you do on stage, if it's not honest, it'll show up phony. So I am what I am when I play a part."

This is the key to his versatility and the answer to what makes him one of the most sought after acts in Vegas. He's appeared eight years on the strip at the Silver Slipper, Circus Circus, the Royal, the Holiday and now the Joker Club. He's been second banana to the best in burlesque including **TOMMY MOE RAFT** and Irving Benson.

In his spare time, Charlie is a tennis buff and was recently made an honorary member of the Sands Tennis Club where he plays almost daily. His favorite partner is Mrs. Lumas, wife of the Summa Corporation president and a "darn good tennis player."

Also opening this week at the Joker Club will be **PATTY WRIGHT** who has just returned from an engagement in Guam.

An all-new show policy featuring go-go dancers and exotics makes its debut at the Jackpot Casino. Two of this towns top exotics open in the show, **SUZETTE SUMMERS** and **GINA BON BON** (pictured).

Vegas Visitor

August 19, 1977 I have been asked numerous times: "How do you become a stripper?"

As with many of today's exotic dancers, I started out as a go-go dancer. My first job was in a small neighborhood type cocktail lounge where I worked six days a week, five hours a day at the then enormous sum of $2.50 an hour. An extra side-benefit of my job was the welcome loss of nearly ten pounds in the first two weeks!

I found that I enjoyed the challenge of spontaneous creativity, creating steps and expressing feelings to songs I had never danced to before. I also enjoyed the applause and the smiles of the customers. On that first job I wore a sexy black Fredericks of Hollywood bikini, which the male customers seemed to appreciate greatly! How times have changed! When is the last time you saw a go-go girl who didn't go topless?

From go-go dancing, I went into chorus line work and eventually back to go-go dancing and then to topless go-go dancing, (I held out for two years and now I can't remember why) and then into exotic dancing. All the time I performed as a go-go dancer, I was adding extras to my show but I didn't know that the extras would eventually be part of my strip show.

I've heard many patrons of the clubs I've worked express the opinion that "all a dancer has to do is shake her ass and take off her clothes. Anyone can do that?"

Well, anyone CAN do that. But that is far from all there is to it. In order to make someone interested enough to watch you shake your booty and take it off; there must be preparation.

Today's shows run from ten to 20 minutes depending on the type of show you're in. I choose my music in tempos not only geared to removing my clothes without falling on my face, but to entertain and keep the audience awake, and to create a theme.

I also choose my costumes with the same thoughts in mind. Since I make my own, this is not too difficult but it does require a lot of time. Things I look for in a costume are sex appeal for the men AND for the women (a burlesque show is often a fashion show for female customers), ease of removal, and a tie-in with the show theme.

An exotic dancer's wardrobe could be considered tools like a carpenter's hammer, a typist's typewriter or a mechanic's wrench. They are designed to do a job and in order to do it well, they must be kept in excellent order. Souvenir seekers should keep this in mind when they make a grab for some little trinket. Each piece we wear has a reason and a missing piece may not only hurt the show but, since we pay for all our own costumes, it hurts our pocketbooks.

As with many exotics, I've added my own touches to burlesque. My wild west magic show is probably my most popular, incorporating country music, magic and a fire show, and climaxing with the production and vanishing of beautiful white doves. I owe this part of the show to magician and partner **TURBAN.**

Vegas Visitor

August 26, 1977 The exotic talents of the beautiful **SUZETTE SUMMERS** (pictured) are being featured as part of the new entertainment policy at the Jackpot Casino along with **GINA BON BON** and a host of exciting topless dancers who dance and serve cocktails.

Suzette, a long-time Las Vegas favorite, began her career at the Hollywood Theatre in San Diego. For 2½ years, she gained experience in every phase of burlesque as she started in the chorus line and found herself thrust into the feature spot when the star of the show became ill. As Suzette puts it, "It was do it or get fired. I didn't even have a costume. I used the one from the opening chorus number."

Suzette went on to become the theatres permanent featured exotic. She learned to do lines for the old burlesque skits, added a bit of singing, and when she felt she was ready, got herself booked into Las Vegas at Paul Perry's old Gay Nineties for New Year's Eve.

From there, Suzette's career quickly shot upward as she starred in several Minsky's shows, worked the finest theatres and nightclubs across the country and returned to Las Vegas to open at the Thunderbird Hotel for three months. This was followed by the Aladdin for two years and on to the Holiday Casino for over a year.

Presently, Suzette is working on her own show and has the makings of a band in OZ and T, who will be backing her as she debuts her singing talents at the Jackpot Casino. "We've made some demo tapes and everyone who's heard them is really excited," says Suzette. "We've even had some offers for concerts!"

Although most of her time is filled with show business related activities, Suzette also has a side line job as a supervisor for Ideal Corporation, specializing in natural skin care products and health aids.

An enthusiast of physical fitness, Suzette enjoys all athletic activities and regularly jogs to keep her 38-23-36 form in top shape. In addition, she studies the benefits of herbology and natural healing.

A Scorpio, Suzette says that although she isn't married now, she believes "that everyone needs a partner for life and that a marriage license is a gift you give to someone you love."

A good cook, she is especially adept at Chinese cooking which she mastered while living in Taiwan for three years.

Born in Charlotte, North Carolina and raised in Longbeach, California, Suzette recalls a birthday card she received at sixteen. "It had a picture of a stripper and some nickels taped to it towards my first costume. I don't even know why they did it. I didn't have any ideas about being a stripper then."

However, it was only a month after graduation that a new exotic talent was added to the ranks of burlesque and since then, Suzette has definitely left her mark everywhere she's appeared.

Burlesque will be losing one of its loveliest performers when **LIZA JOURDAN** of the Cabaret retires this month to set up housekeeping with Timothy James Logan (brother of **LOVIE GOLDMINE**). According to Liza: "We're moving to Paradise Tahoe where I'm trading my G-string for a fishing line and tackle."

Magician-comedian **TURBAN** is back at the Cabaret by popular demand. Artie Brooks has returned to the runways of the amateur nude dance contest at the Palomino.

Lots of movies are being made around Las Vegas right now and many of the local entertainers are working as extras. They include **BOB MITCHELL, DEXTER MAITLAND, TURBAN,** Oscar Cartier, **CIMMARON, CHRISTINE DARLING, SUZI MIDNIGHT, GINA BON BON** and **JONI JANSEN.**

Vegas Visitor

September 2, 1977 Attention ladies! **ARTIE BROOKS** (pictured), comedy star of the Palomino Club, is looking for a wife! Applicants should apply in person any night at the Palomino. Ladies should be between 18-35, 5' to 5'5" leaning toward the plump rather than the skinny side.

Artie says he is a leg man. "They must have two. And I like well-formed thighs."

He also requires a homebody type. "I need a woman, who is a good housewife and cook to love me, take care of me, and inspire me to greater heights." ("How tall do you want to be?" asks **SUSI MIDNIGHT**).

Although Artie is the first to donate his time to help underprivileged children, he doesn't want any of his own "because they're nothing more than short dumb people!"

In return for the above qualifications, Artie is a bit stumped on what he has to offer. "This might blow it," he admits. "It'll be a very shabby existence with many sacrifices on HER part. She'll wear the same Levies every day. I also have a fireplace and a washer and dryer in my apartment. I'll give her faithfulness. I'm warm and kind and gentle. I have an old "paid for" '69 Cadillac. But it's a convertible. And I am generous. She'll have the best Levi's with all the trimmings, not those J.C. Penney's plain pockets. With me, it's first class!"

"She'll also have the benefit of my wisdom, my high degree of intellect, my worldly experience, my dictionary, and my great and surprised appreciation if anyone falls for all of this!"

Artie has been in the limelight over 30 years starting as a singer with big bands and gradually working in his funny ad-libs and jokes as he developed the comic style that entertains so many today. He had a big head start having been born in the proverbial trunk as his mother and father toured the country with a song and dance routine in the vaudeville days.

Asked how a comic gets started today, Artie shrugs and says, "It's really tough. There used to be dozens of clubs using comics. Now the few that do, use guys with ten or twenty years experience. There are a few places that have special showcases like the Comedy Store in Hollywood or the Sahara Showcase here in Las Vegas, but the opportunities are slim. I advise a would-be comic to develop his own style, to avoid copying television comics and to keep trying. If you're determined enough and good enough, you'll make it."

Artie sees a return of comedy to the burlesque scene. "I think a sex-orientated show must have humor to be truly successful. It has to be tongue-in-cheek."

Artie has seen lots of changes in burlesque over the years. "Years ago the girls didn't go any further than their bra and pants and the guys loved it. I think the thing that hurt burlesque the most was electronic music. It helped eliminate the emcees that gave the bands their breaks. It took the drive out of the girl's shows too. It eliminated a lot of their creativity. When something is canned it gets to be routine, the spontaneity is gone."

There is no warm-up routine for Artie before he steps on stage. He is instantly on. "The minute I step out there something happens. Everything else is left behind. I always do my shows cold sober – no booze, no pills. That would slow me down rather than stimulate me and it would stifle my creativity."

An avid photographer in his spare time, Artie takes pictures of all the girls who work at the Palomino and between the professionals and the hundreds of amateurs who have passed through the last three years, he's probably taken thousands of pictures; an enviable collection even for *Playboy Magazine*.

He is also a nostalgia buff and enjoys music from the 30s. Chess is on his list of hobbies too. A sports enthusiast, Artie has a golf handicap of 12 and a bowling average of 215.

Quick to donate his time on behalf of charitable causes, he is also on the jester's panel of Saints and Sinners.

And ladies, all joking aside, Artie IS looking for the right girl to marry. For the right girl, there will be quite a guy! Personally, I think Artie is still looking for someone like his exotic star ex-wife **BAMBI JONES** (pictured).

JESS MACK relates an interesting anecdote: One night a few years ago, he and his lovely wife **DOROTHY** were celebrating his birthday at the Aladdin watching the burlesque show starring **TOMMY MOE RAFT**. Tommy presented Jess with his "lucky" keno ticket and told Jess that was his birthday present. Jess played it and won $2200.00!

Vegas Visitor

September 9, 1977 On my day off last week, I took a special flight to Scottsdale, Arizona on a Piper Cherokee piloted by **JAN FONTAINE** (pictured), one of the featured exotics, at the Joker Club and Arlene Brooks, a dealer at the Hacienda.

We left about seven in the morning, a beautiful clear day, no wind and still cool. Jan and I were in fine shape from no sleep since Saturday but that was all right because Arlene was flying us in.

I never realized just how barren much of the country is between here and Phoenix and when you do spot a settlement in the middle of nowhere, you wonder how it got there. Arlene was well prepared for the trip with a map in her lap which she assured me was not "just for looks." However, as we neared Scottsdale, I began to wonder as Jan and Arlene tried to decide where the airport could be. "It must be here somewhere." "I don't see it." "Call the tower." "Let's just circle one more time. It has to be here somewhere."

Just as they were about to call the tower, they spotted the tiny Scottsdale airstrip, and began the descent. "The left strut is broken." "Are you sure?" "Yes, I'm sure. That's going to make it harder to land."

Worried, I looked at the wing. It was still there. The engine was still going. I didn't even ask what a strut was. I didn't want to know.

After our landing, which was smoother than any of the recent commercial flights I've taken, the girls explained that a strut was stuck and it made landing like trying to steer with a flat tire. As we crossed the airstrip, they kept congratulating each other on finding the airport. They told me that this is the biggest problem in flying because you don't know what to look for.

We spent our time in Scottsdale as the guests of Nancy Bowles, formerly a nightclub owner and now partners with her mother in a gift shop specializing in home made crafts. She congratulated us

on the first junket from Las Vegas as we all loaded up on items we couldn't live without. There was even debate on whether there would be room left for me on our return flight!

A shopping spree at the Metro, Phoenix newest and largest two story mall, was a must on our agenda, as well as a bit of sightseeing which involved only one museum, the rest of the time was spent just looking at all the beautiful homes.

Evening brought us to Granny's, a home cooking and home-style eating establishment in Scottsdale. After Arlene wrote down everything she ate on a list as directed by her hypnotist, so he could red-circle everything that was a no no, she continued to entertain us by causing a shower of toothpicks to rain upon the lobby when she tried to push the bar on the dispenser.

We finished the night with a trip to the Hilton, where we were quickly cut off from any possibilities by a group of 12 other women. Never choose a corner table next to a wall. We did nearly lure a stray dog into the back seat of the car as we left!

All in all it was a most entertaining trip, mostly due to the company. Life can't be dull with a comedienne like Arlene, the bubbly Jan and the warm friendship of Nancy and her lovely mother.

Not only has Robert Scott Hooper, photographer extraordinaire for the Vegas Visitor, captured the centerfold of this month's *Playboy Magazine* but he also has another feature pictorial in next months issue including the ravishing **DIEDRE RHODES** from the Cabaret.

A special thanks to Mark Tan, Forest Duke, **P.J.** and **JIM PARKER**, who worked on behalf of the many burlesque entertainers, for getting us our first opportunity to vote in the annual Las Vegas Entertainment Awards. P.J. and Jim tell me that they also tried for a special burlesque category and although they weren't successful this year, it is on the agenda for another try next year. There are many super talented people in the burlesque field and it is time for them to have the recognition they've worked so hard to earn. Some of the other entertainers and some of the public forget that many of today's biggest stars got their start in burlesque including Jackie Gleason, Phil Silvers, and **JOEY BISHOP.** Even Goldie Hawn started as a go-go dancer!

Vegas Visitor

September 16, 1977 The second time around is even better than the first when you see the fabulous "Casino de Paris," a Frederic Apcar production at the Dunes Hotel.

The production numbers, staged and choreographed by Ron Lewis, are some of the most spectacular in the world, with dazzling wardrobe designed by Jose Luis Vinas. The Jon Lexia Orchestra provides the vibrant musical accompaniment, which is so important to this thoroughly enjoyable show.

Each of the specialty acts is preceded by a grand introduction number carrying out the theme of the act to follow such as the "Colonial American Salute" depicting the charm and elegance of an era unfortunately all but forgotten with its elegantly dressed men and women. The Independence Ball brings on the star of the show, superb English styled comic Freddie Sales. His elegant manner of speech and beautiful British accent, coupled with outlandish humor clothed in the most formal of old time English, is a most original and entertaining treat.

The Fercos performed in two spots in the show, the first with a fantastic juggling act. Consisting of two brothers and two sisters, they combine superb showmanship and humor. They amaze the audience with their dexterity in a variety of juggling antics with flying discs, ping pong balls shot to the ceiling from their mouths and bowling pins juggled over, around and in-between each other.

They return in a later segment with the aid of their mother and father to provide some breathtaking flying acrobatics.

The Stupid's from Stockholm also provide some clowning acrobatic antics complete with baggy pants in the best of the circus traditions.

Singer Ginnie Pallone offers musical moments to remember with such selections as "When I Found You" and the popular "Love Will Keep Us Together."

Offering a variety of production numbers, the Ron Lewis Dancers give the audience a view of several exciting and spectacular scenes varying from the Egyptian scene complete with a real "Leo" to their very French and sexy finale. A must for all show goers.

It is always a treat to have visiting magicians stop in to chat with me at the Joker Club. This past week, J. Marlboro, author of a book on magic and Michael Brazill, owner of Rings & Things, dropped in to catch my show and offered me several interesting tips as well as some appreciated encouragement. Mr. Marlboro opens this week at the Magic Castle near Los Angeles.

Performing the world's only "strip-o-rama" at the Cabaret is the exciting **CARMEN HOLIDAY** (pictured). One of the country's top exotics, Carmen explains the shows as "play-lets intended to share some of my most intimate sexual fantasies!" These scenarios include "The Obscene Phone Call," "Diary of a Chambermaid," and "The Happy Hooker." The titles alone should tempt you into a visit.

THE VELVET ODESSEY is making preparations for a European tour. The beautiful brunette has been busy adding new wardrobe and new routines to an already varied performance. See her at the world famous Palomino Club.

Late item: Opening this week at the Palomino is "The Heavenly Body," **TERI STARR,** internationally known exotic performer. In addition to performances all over the world, Teri has also appeared in several major motion pictures as well as dozens of television shows and commercials. After her Las Vegas appearance, Teri will be heading once again to Europe for another extensive tour by popular demand.

Vegas Visitor

September 23, 1977   Please accept my personal invitation to visit me at the Joker's Club in North Las Vegas, where I appear nightly in "Jokers Wild Burlesque," starring two of the funniest comics in burlesque, **BOB MITCHELL** and **CHARLIE VESPIA.** From the outset, the show was designed to bring the audience back to the days of old time burlesque with the baggy pants comics and the inane antics of the cast acting out the classic skits, sometimes corny, a bit outlandish at times, and always funny.

We have a lot of repeat customers. They never get bored because the scenes are never done exactly the same way twice. Sometimes a customer will see the show all three times in the same night just to catch the hilarious improvisations of **BOB MITCHELL** and **CHARLIE VESPIA.**

Of course, the show has its full complement of the female species including talking woman and exotic **CHRISTINE DARLING, JAN FONTAINE** with her new "Star Wars" show, and **PATTY WRIGHT** who never fails to enlist all eligible young men as she does her "Salute to America As Uncle Sam."

An interesting note: Patty just took delivery of the first 1978 Mark V sold this year. Of course, no one will talk to her now!

Word has it that **SUZETTE SUMMERS** has joined the cast of "Rare 'N Bare" at the Royal Las Vegas. She's the perfect addition!

CARMEN HOLIDAY and **SATAN'S ANGEL** (pictured), share feature billing at the Jackpot Casino.

ANGELIQUE PETTYHOHN (pictured) is performing a new show called the "Marquis de Sade" at the Cabaret. This, in addition to her "Cabaret," and "French" shows, gives her audience quite a sample of her versatility.

VALERIE RAE CLARK, recent Penthouse cover girl who appeared at the Cabaret just a few months back, wrote me from her home in Alhambra, California to announce that she is expecting a baby. The father is her choreographer George Fullwood. There must be a million lines about the "steps" he was teaching her. Anyway, congratulations Valerie!

Vegas Visitor

October 7, 1977 The biggest attraction in North Las Vegas is the world-famous Palomino Club and one of its biggest attractions is the infamous **BARBIE DOLL** (pictured).

One of her many fans is Jimmy Walker (J.J. on "Good Times"). Could some of his new lines come from sitting at the runway during one of Barbie's performances? And there is Debbie Reynolds, who said "just great." Doc Severinsen said, "She's the healthiest looking heifer I've ever seen. " The Carpenters wanted to take her home! And Jack Albertson summed Barbie's show up when he said he'd never seen someone have such complete command over an audience.

Customers don't rise from their seats when Barbie's on stage because she sees everything and comments on everything.

A trip to the bathroom can conjure up every possible intention except the innocent one and all very publicly.

Everyone gets a chance to participate, willingly or unwillingly, in Barbie's show as she snaps a big wicked black whip in the air, which immediately discourages any unwanted ad libbing on the customer's part. She lets them unzip and unhook her and then she pulls an unsuspecting young man up from the audience and begins to undress him (shirt only) although she could get the rest with no extra effort and makes him don a jock strap with a tassel, urging him to try out for the part of her Tarzan! It's all in fun and when she assists the man off the stage, he walks just a little taller and with the biggest smile in the house and possibly more!

It wouldn't be fair to quote Barbie's lines here but suffice it to say she uses many of the commercials in her shows with their tag lines aptly adapted to the risqué humor only Barbie can deliver. And though Barbie is a beautiful well-built (36-24-36) blonde, she is one of the few strippers about whom a customer can truthfully say, "I love her mind. It's so funny." Few and far between is the customer who can keep up with Barbie. I believe she'd even give Don Rickles a run for his money.

As if being a topnotch comedy stripper weren't enough, Barbie is also an talented country singer. She's already cut one record: "He's Everything to Me." She will soon be signed to Crème Records under the management of Dusty Rhodes. She's worked professionally singing and touring with the Bobby Durham Show. Someday the country music field may steal one of the most talented girls in burlesque then watch out Minnie Pearl, Dolly Parton and Tanya Tucker.

Barbie tells me she got her start in the exotic field in Cleveland because her first husband used to go out on her with "blonde go-go girls. So I bleached my hair blonde and got my first job as a go-go girl. Then I got rid of him."

Barbie was the top draw in Cleveland for more than five years and went into burlesque six months after her first go-go job. Mr. Jess Myers of the Roxie Theatre hired her right off the stage. She remembers him as saying "What the h--- are you doing go-go dancing when you could be a stripper so easily?" She went to work for him the following week and only five weeks later became a feature attraction on the East coast theatre circuit.

I remember following her into the Follies Theatre in New York City and hearing all the talk about the wild Barbie. No one could follow her and that week's feature was no exception. Barbie was booked back as often as her schedule would permit which was mostly divided between New York City and Boston.

She's particularly proud of having worked with a couple of the giants in burlesque comedy, Willie Dew and the East's top banana, Scurvey Miller.

Four years ago, Barbie was booked into the Palomino on a four-week contract with a two-week option. She's still working that two-week option!

Barbie likes the change of faces at the Palomino. "It's like working a new club every day. I don't get bored. I love the beautiful staging and lights. I have everything I need to do the best job I can." And she does exactly that, every night at the Palomino. Drop in and say hi, if you dare!

Vegas Visitor

October 14, 1977 Elegantly costumed in sparkling rhinestones and feather-laden headdresses, beautiful redheaded **BAMBI LEIGH** (pictured), reveals her true-to-life Playboy Bunny form of 38-24-35, nightly at the Cabaret. Bambi, who started her dancing career as a go-go dancer in Oklahoma, keeps the same high pitch of energy in her performance as an exotic.

Crediting a dancer from Minsky's and a dancer from the famous June Taylor troupe with giving her a push in the right direction, Bambi has since performed all over the United States, spending most of her time in cities such as Boston, New York and Montreal. Bambi says her own true love is fellow traveler "Teddy Bear," a huge Manute Husky!

Another new face at the Cabaret is **TRIXIE** (pictured), who came to Las Vegas bringing with her a host of beauty titles including Miss Nude Teenager of 1974, Miss Nude Canada 1975 and first runner up to Miss Nude Universe.

Trixie got her start in the exotic field five years ago when she applied for a job as a cocktail waitress in Nashville, Tennessee. There were no openings for waitresses but they did need an exotic. Trixie gave it a try and has been dancing ever since!

Still looking like a 19 year old Miss Nude Teenager, Trixie glides across the stage and performs her strip in the tradition of Gypsy Rose Lee, as she portrays the fair damsel in "Old Fashioned Love Song." She also has a special little girl show guaranteed to make any man in the audience volunteer for the role of "Daddy."

Anyone would agree that a man going to a discount massage parlor and finding it a do-it yourself operation certainly isn't getting any respect! That is just one of the zany stories told by Rodney "I don't get no respect" Dangerfield. "From the day I was born, I didn't get any respect," claims Rodney. "When I was born, they slapped my mother!"

Rodney's hour long show at the Tropicana is filled with some of the funniest material I've ever heard in Las Vegas. He never gave the audience a chance to stop laughing before he zinged them with another one. We all loved him.

Singer Gail Baker opened Rodney's show with a selection of songs showing her marvelous vocal range. The audience and I were especially delighted with her selection from "Chorus Line."

I also had a chance to catch a few of Chris Fio Rito's numbers in the lounge.

Vegas Visitor

October 21, 1977 The big news this week is the moving of the "Joker's Wild Burlesque" show to the Cabaret Burlesque Palace as a special treat for daytime burlesque fans. The show has been lengthened to two hours with six exotics and old time burlesque skits with **BOB MITCHELL** and **CHARLIE VESPIA**. It will be a continuous show beginning at 2:30PM with the last show at 6:30PM. The evening line-up of exotics and emcee **TURBAN** will be following the last show.

The daytime show will include **CHRISTINE DARLING** who will perform exotic routines as well as the main straight woman in the burlesque skits. Also featured are **JAN FON-**

I've seen him twice and both times he's had a full room with lots of people standing around the edges, clapping and joining in to sing their favorite song.

TAINE, ANGLIQUE PETTYJOHN, AMARETTA and the lithe acrobatics of **TRIANA ZZON**. I will be adding my touch of magic to the show.

SUSI MIDNIGHT (pictured with Liberace at Palomino Club) "The Flame of the Jet Set" numbers among many fans, the incomparable **LIBERACE**. Actually it is also the other way around. Susi makes it a point to attend every Liberace opening, extols his virtues endlessly letting everyone know that Liberace is at the top of her list. Liberace responds in kind, by attending the shows at the Palomino where Susi does her usual spicy number to special tapes of piano selections by Liberace, of course!

Special visitors Roland Muse, one of the country's top burlesque agents from Miami (he's my agent, too!) and Mike Pinter of Club Juana in Orlando stopped by the Joker Club to say hi and then stopped across the street to the Palomino to catch Artie Brooks and the amateur nude dance contest followed by the big exotic show. Mike said he was especially impressed with the wild **BARBIE DOLL** and Roland wanted to start booking the **VELVET ODESSEY** yesterday!

Birthday greetings go out this month to **SNOWY SINCLAIR, TURBAN,** and **TEX** at the Cabaret, Gary at the Joker Club and to one of my own little girls – Catherine who just turned a very grown-up seven years old.

Vegas Visitor

October 28, 1977 Seldom does an exotic enter the field with as much preparation and planning as 34C-24-34 **AMARETTA** (pictured), specifically designed around the art of strip tease.

Amaretta started her career in Denver at the Chez Paree, where with the help of the five girls on the show, she was gowned and groomed and put on stage with no prior experience.

"I stayed about three months. I made up my mind that I wanted to be really good and I was going to go where the best training was available and I decided that had to be Las Vegas."

In Las Vegas, Amaretta worked two days a week at the Jolly Trolley in order to pay choreographer Manfree Manor to teach her to work with fans and to give her some professional dance steps to adapt to her strip routine. She took lessons in theatrical make-up from Mai Ling Hoffman and had her gowns designed by Steve Day.

All this she accomplished in about a years time. "I went to dance classes three times a week and then I practiced what I learned at the Jolly Trolley until I thought I was ready."

An audition with **PAUL PERRY** at the Palomino landed her an immediate job and she has since worked for him at the Palomino, the Joker Club and is now appearing in the daytime show at the Cabaret.

Amaretta was born in Palermo, Sicily. She came to the United States as a child and was raised in Pittsfield, Massachusetts. Before entering the burlesque field she spent much of her time traveling. She lived for a while in Cuernavaca, Mexico where she picked up some of the Spanish language. She also speaks some Italian and says she would like to be more fluent in both.

Her hobbies include abstract painting. "My boyfriend says they're awful," she admits. Her macramé is good enough to sell and she has taken up photography.

She also helps Keith Evans in training wild animals including the black panther **LUCY** in the picture. Amaretta plans to take her show on the road for a while and then to eventually make Las Vegas her permanent home.

How does she like her new career? "I love the glamour of it, the clothes, the stage, the lights, and the applause. I want to keep improving, to take more dance training and maybe even some drama classes."

Vegas Visitor

November 11, 1977 **KITTEN, MISS NUDE UNIVERSE** (pictured), is currently giving the patrons of the Cabaret a sample of the form that won

her the coveted title and has since brought her fame as a top attraction all across the country and more recently as a movie star!

Kitten, with her 40-20-34 dimensions, was recently seen in the Russ

Myer film "Up" which played in Las Vegas at the El Portal. She played the part of an English damsel who narrated the sexy film.

You will see her again in the starring role in "Beneath the Valley of the Ultra Vixen," another Russ Meyer production. "But this one is quite a bit different from his usual films," explains Kitten. "He's gotten criticism in the past for the violence in some of his films. This one is a slapstick sexy comedy with no violence."

Kitten, who helped write the script, plays duo roles in the film. She plays a hillbilly with a southern drawl and a Spanish lass with a Spanish accent.

"It's really a challenge to my abilities as an actress. It helps that a lot of the script is based on my own hilarious sexual escapades."

If you want to catch some of Kitten's "in person" sexiness, hurry to the Cabaret and bring a towel. She takes a bath in a clear champagne glass and much of the audience enjoys the sudsing!

It's always fun to work with someone you've worked with before. This week I have the pleasure of working with **DELILAH JONES** (pictured) in the day show at the Cabaret.

Delilah and I last worked together at the Tender Trap in Phoenix, Arizona and our paths have crossed across the country several times since, not quite meeting, each opening or closing in a club minutes after the other!

Delilah, a former Miss Germany, has added some new material to her act, namely some unbelievable body contortions, along with a lot of beautiful wardrobe that she designed and made herself.

Californians may recognize Delilah from the Body Shop in Hollywood where she appeared several years. She just returned to the States from Canada where she appeared in all the top nightspots in cities such as Montreal and Toronto.

Fans of the fantastic **TURBAN** will be happy to know that he is currently appearing at the all-new Diamond Jim's (formerly Guys and Dolls). Turban, with his magic and mirth, will be heading an all-star cast of exotics including **LIBERTY WEST, JONI JANSEN, CIMMARON**, and Lynn opening tonight. The club will also be featuring daytime go-go dancers for your enjoyment seven days a week. They are still looking for dancers, so if you are interested stop in and talk to Turban.

Mako Ota is back at the Palomino after a long visit back to her homeland of Japan.

I was very fortunate to catch the closing night show at Le Café starring **PATRICK** "The All American Male Stripper" (pictured). He was every bit as exciting as my friends **ANGELIQUE PETTYJOHN** and **TRIANA ZZON** had been telling me. He had the ladies eating right out of his hand and touching anywhere they could! It was a very masculine performance of what used to be strictly female territory. I say equal rights for men. Let's see what they've been bragging about so long! And if they all looked like Patrick, every woman would be back for seconds.

Co-starring in the same show was the incredible Mr. Maury Richards. I know he is a female impersonator, but it is the first time I have ever heard such a performer sing LIVE. And what a voice. He is incomparable. Mr. Richards stands with the likes of Shirley Bassey, Diana Ross, and Lena Horne. But she is a he and there is nothing close to Mr. Richards. If there had been room to stand at the Le Café, he would have had a dozen standing ovations. As it was, the audience was sitting on air instead of chairs. Watch for his album "All By Myself" on the Casa Blanca label to be released soon.

Big David performed a fabulous imitation of Totie Fields. Marge is to be congratulated on a super show.

Strippers with nice wardrobe who are interested in performing in Mexico City and Monterey should call Gypsy Louise. The contract is for two months at

$650 per week, room and air transporta-

tion provided.

Vegas Visitor

November 18, 1977 Diamond Jim's, formerly Guys and Dolls, opened last Thursday night with a special invitation to cab drivers, the press, and all the entertainers to come and partake of a fabulous spare rib buffet, sparkling champagne, and live entertainment, all on the house. I was accompanied by most of the day show at the Cabaret and we immediately sniffed out the vittles and settled down to having someone entertain us after a hard days grind (don't pardon the expression as it is apropos in burlesque)!

We were treated to some of the best go-go dancers I've ever seen. They were all pretty and they can ALL dance, which is saying more than some may realize. I've worked with probably a thousand go-go girls and if one could really dance, she was an exception. At Diamond Jim's they can ALL dance.

Interspersed throughout the go-go entertainment, the lovely redhead and extremely agile Cimmaron displayed her exotic charms in the first 20 minute show I've ever seen her do. I've seen Cimmaron at the Royal Las Vegas several times and she was always great but Thursday night she outdid herself and the audience responded in kind.

LOU DALEY and **LENA ROMA-NO** furnished the novelty spot for the evening, combining song, dance, comedy and striptease. Lena's bright green teddy bear stole the show!

The Jerry Jackson Dancers earn their bread and butter in the all-new "Pinups 2001" at the Sahara. Especially strenuous was the "Working at the Car Wash" number. I've never seen a car wash with that much activity!

The opening of the 2001 show is a must see just for its dramatic effect and certainly sets the theme for this out of the world show.

Imagine clouds of eerie fog seeping from under the curtain and as the curtain rises, you see six space people dressed in stark white jumpsuits and space helmets. The jumpsuits are quickly ripped off and the girls begin the exciting fast pace of the show, which never lets up.

Celine Britt is a highly talented combination of dancer and singer. I'm always happy when I hear a really good singer or watch a really good dancer, but when I see the combination in one person, I'm awed!

Peter Anthony was so funny as he stood on stage, bumping the microphone with his nose, telling his wacky stories. I never did understand the one about Glen Miller and Bing Crosby. I was sure he'd get that nose caught in his trumpet, which by the way he can really play. I would have liked to hear him do a whole song through instead of those K-Tel specials.

For years I've head about the "Jewel Box Revue" which is now appearing at the Carrousel De Paris. And like most shows you've hard a lot about, I expected a lot. In this case, I got more!

The show is about an hour and a half long and features some of the best female impersonators I've ever seen. Although no one really "looks" like the famous people they portray, with the exception of the Carol Channing, the mannerisms and the excitement of the real thing were all there. I 'saw' Liza Minnelli romp through a bit of "Cabaret." I enjoyed a marvelously choreographed "If My Friends Could See Me Now" a la Shirley MacLaine, a soul stirring Diana Ross, and a marvelous Barbra Streisand.

Even more fun though, was the beautiful and poignant "Isn't It Rich?" enhanced with the antics of three clowns; the Jewel Box Dancers. They also lend their considerable talents to most of the numbers in the revue.

Vegas Visitor

November 25, 1977 From Port Arthur, Texas, comes a lovely former doctor's assistant, **CINNAMON STEEN** (pictured), to lend her fantastic dance talents to the "Pinups 2001 Show," at the Sahara.

Cinnamon told me that she's had no formal dancing training. "It's a gift," she says. And she works overtime making that gift pay as she performs in 11 of the 17 numbers in the show. Every number requires so much stamina that during the first nights of the show an oxygen tank was kept backstage for the exhausted dancers.

"After a while, you get in shape and you can pace yourself," explained Cinnamon and then the oxygen tanks are taken away. "What was really hard is having to learn all of those routines in 17 days."

The routines Cinnamon speaks of include a cheerleader number that leads into a boogie-woogie and a special number to "Car Wash" with barely enough time between numbers to blink an eye, let alone take a breath.

Further proof of Cinnamon's talent is the winning of the Ensemble Girl of the Year award in 1974 while performing in "Bare Touch of Vegas."

She also worked with **SAMMY DAVIS JR.** on his road show and went from that to a concert tour with Issac Hayes. Cinnamon has appeared several times on television lending her dancing talents to the Mary Tyler Moore Special, Mike Douglas Show, Johnny Carson Show, and the Merv Griffin show.

Once again, illustrating how paths cross, I first saw Cinnamon perform with the Al Belo show at the Mapes Hotel in Reno.

Cinnamon demonstrates quite a knack for comedy as she mugs her way through the revival number in the Pinups show as well as adding other sparks of light and humor to what is a top-notch show.

A sleeping bit of dynamite is exploding at the Maxim in the dancing review "Maxim Force" starring **BILL FAN-NING**. Taking you on an intergalactic journey, this revue includes some original numbers choreographed by Shirley Freeman. I don't say original lightly either. Each dance sequence has a special touch and isn't a replica of the other shows on the Strip. Especially outstanding is the convicts number and a

mirror number with a live dancing reflection.

There is also a unique adagio dance team in the revue, which combines the artistry and grace of the ballroom adagio with some insane comedy wherein the couple takes some hilarious falls.

Congratulations go to Jimmy Wise, the costume designer, for some very simple but elegant wardrobe in keeping with the space theme and also revealing enough of the dancers forms that you can appreciate their looks and their dancing talents.

This marvelous futuristic space review was produced and directed by Jim Wallace and co-produced and written by J.C. Curtis. Show times are at ten and midnight.

Country music fans will be happy to know that the Bobby Durham Show is now appearing at the fabulous Joker Club in North Las Vegas. The Joker Club has been completely remodeled to include a large dance floor, booths and tables enough to seat everyone, but with the intimacy that will be sure to promote a little fooling around! And Bobby is eager to play all of your requests to get that special someone in the mood.

JUDY MICHAELS has joined the cast of the new Diamond Jim's across the street from the MGM. There is also an amateur topless contest every Monday night and entertainment manager, host, emcee, comedian, magician, window washer **TURBAN,** is inviting all young ladies to participate and compete for cash prizes including a $50 first prize.

Just returning from a sensational Canadian engagement is popular Palomino comedy star **ARTIE BROOKS**. Big things are in the future for Artie too, as he is already signed to some four-figure, one-night concert bookings. Congratulations!

SUSI MIDNIGHT, also appearing at the Palomino, is creating quite a buzz in Las Vegas with her recent debut as a burlesque columnist. Welcome to my world, Susi!

Vegas Visitor

December 2, 1977 The most spectacular line-up of exotic talent in the world make their debut every afternoon on the runways of the Palomino and Cabaret clubs at 2PM continuous until 4:30 AM. Some of the exotics at the two clubs are pictured here as they make preparations for scheduled performances. Our Flight Captain is licensed pilot/exotic **JAN FONTAINE,** of Fontaine Airlines – and her crew includes yours truly, claiming distinction as backseat navigator. All of the girls invite you aboard for a trip out of this world!

Our photographer was Steve Miller who is a licensed fight instructor and owner of the two airplanes in the photo. Photography is his favorite sideline second only to? If you'd like instruction, in flying that is, you can call him.

Pictured from the left are **ANGLIQUE, TERRY THOMAS, VELVET ODEYSSEY, JODY ENGLISH, DELILAH JONES, JAN FONTAINE, TERI STARR,** and **DUSTY SUMMERS.**

The best entertainment in town can be found in the lounge shows all over Las Vegas and at reasonable prices too, usually under $1.50 for a drink and a one-drink minimum. I made the rounds of a few of these shows recommended to me by friends and I'd like to recommend them to you.

First on my list were the Goofers in the Lounge at the Landmark. These

Italian style entertainers, formerly with Louis Prima, deliver a non-stop show packed with comedy, music and more comedy. This is a group you've got to see to believe with tunes such as "I Nevah Promised Youa a Rosa Garden" and the special comedy interpretation of what a singer is REALLY thinking when he's singing that romantic ballad.

I also caught the last of the Tom Christie show in the same lounge. What a voice and he's good looking too. He extended his thanks to the Summa Corporation for getting him a spot on the Merv Griffin Show, which in turn has netted him several television and movie offers.

Bobby Douglas was in his final week at the Royal Inn. He does some great Elvis impersonations and has a beautiful recording in "The King Is Gone." Bobby is also adept at audience contact via his expressive eyes and face.

Several months ago my friend

GEORGETTE DANTE told me about the fabulous Perfecto and Motion at the Circus Circus. She said I had to go see them. Finally my schedule permitted and all she said was true. Perfecto adapts his musical talents to whatever his audience is in the mood for and requests are the meat of the show. In one set they did a Waylon Jennings "Basics of Life," "Look of Love," "Birth of the Blues," "Chicago," and "Don't It Make My Brown Eyes Blue."

Diamond Jim's has Las Vegas' only nude upside down stripper in the person of Laurie Thomas. She's also an extremely agile young lady on her feet. Also new in the show is Amber Delaney, direct from Canada.

"Olde Tyme Burlesque" skits have been moved from the day show at the Cabaret to the night show. The day show will continue with a bevy of beautiful exotics starting at 2PM.

Vegas Visitor

December 9, 1977   Headlining at the Jolly Trolley is vivacious **CASSANDRA LEE** (pictured), who has starred recently in a number of first class burlesque productions in Las Vegas, Reno, and on the road with Minsky's. She also won the celebrity look a-like portion of the Beaux Arts Ball for her Liza Minnelli, which you can still see in one of her three performances nightly at the Trolley.

You may also have seen Cassandra on television where she's appeared on the Dick Maurice Show, The Brothers Show, and I happened to catch her on a rerun of the Fourth Unoffficial Miss Las Vegas Showgirl Pageant where she represented the Silver Slipper.

CHELSEA DAYE (Miss Nude America 1976-77 pictured) opened this week at Diamond Jim's. Held over is Shamash Lee, a versatile exotic with a variety of shows all on the lighter side with great touches of comedy as well as plenty of sexiness!

Vegas Visitor

December 23, 1977 The red-headed sophisticated lady gracefully dancing her way down the runway of the Palomino every afternoon is world renown exotic, actress, **TERI STARR** (pictured). Known as "The Heavenly Body," Teri's 38½-24-36 measurements quickly capture audience imagination as they enjoy her elegant and sensuous approach to the art of striptease.

TERI STARR

Teri is also a licensed beautician, a former dance instructor for Arthur Murray, and a gym instructor. She got her start in the exotic world with a two-week stint as a go-go dancer in Los Angeles. "I soon found out that all that go-go stuff wasn't my cup of tea," says Teri, wherein she began performing her own specialty numbers working her training as a ballroom dancer and her gymnastic abilities into her routines.

Teri has travelled all over the world and performed in such exotic spots as the Hilton and Sheridan Hotels in Egypt,

Quebec City, Canada, and her favorite country Japan.

She was especially impressed with the elegance of the nightclubs in Japan and the beautiful manners of the men in the club. "I felt safe everywhere I went."

One of the clubs she worked in sat only eight customers and had four hostesses, a bartender, a "Mamasan" and Teri as the entertainer. "The interior was gorgeous with thick plush carpeting, rich wall hangings, and a beautiful crystal chandelier. The club was no bigger than the dressing room here at the Palomino. When I came out to dance, the tables they had their drinks on folded up and I danced on the bar."

How much did all this luxury cost a customer? "I was told," says Teri, "that you couldn't leave without spending at least a hundred dollars and there was a waiting list to get in."

While in Japan, Teri did a television documentary on how an American viewed Japan and some television commercials for Japanese products including one for Tao Jewelry. "For that one I had to speak Japanese which I don't. They held up cards for me to read phonetically."

In the states, Teri has had several bit parts for Universal and MGM Pictures as well as larger roles on the television series "Police Woman" and "Police Story" and a number of commercials.

Teri enjoys road travel. "The road puts pressure on you to do a good show because you're usually the only entertainer in the show. I enjoy working in some comedy, some audience participation, my dancing and just a lot of variety. I really love entertaining. The only disadvantage to the road is you often don't have the right staging and lights for what you want to do."

In her spare time, Teri enjoys reading books on self-improvement. She's finishing "The Complete Book of Running." She is interested in books on the world of finance and wants to learn as much as she can about economics.

Teri has studied real estate and decided against being a salesman. "It was interesting but the more I got into it the more I realized I wasn't the salesman type."

Right now, Teri is going to poker dealing school, eventually planning to become a dealer "unless I change my mind and go to Europe!"

Note: Patrick, "The All American Male Stripper," vacationing in Florida writes me that he opens in Breck Wall's new show in Dallas soon.

I wish to extend my personal sympathy to Tex Marshall of the Cabaret and his family in the loss of his beautiful wife Martha. Those who knew her will be missing that extra ray of sunshine.

It also saddens me to hear of the death of Mr. Carmichael, my former boss and friend at Surfside Seven in Ft. Walton Beach. It's hard to believe that someone so close is no longer with us.

Vegas Visitor

December 30, 1977 It's time once again to make those New Year's resolutions; - the promises you are determined to keep at least until January 2. I asked the following friends for their New Year's resolutions. Some of them were surprising, some were a bit odd, most of them were just fun. Hope you enjoy them all.

I started with the newest professional in the day show at the Palomino. Chanel brings her sexy discotheque styling direct from the winner's circle of the nighttime amateur show where she's been a consistent winner. The dark-haired Cuban beauty says: "I'd like to bring my grandmother here from Cuba to live with me."

Cherry: "I resolve to quit stripping – by age 90."

Tina Lane – "I resolve to quit biting my nails. I also resolve to live with a man at least a year before marriage."

ARTIE BROOKS – "I resolve to sell all my polo ponies because I don't think they are happy in my apartment."

BARBIE DOLL – "I'm not going to sky dive anymore. That's the same thing I give up for lent. I also promise not to sing any more soul music."

SUSI MIDNIGHT – "I'm going to start dating again."

Terry Van Sans – "I'd like to lose 15 pounds. Maybe if I make that public, I'll stick to it."

From the Gilded Cage: April Maitland – "I want to be a successful dancer."

From the Joker Club: Margie Regenhardt – I'd like to spend more time with friends I have right here in town who work different shifts than I do." (Side note) Congratulations to Margie's son Bill on his recent performance as the bartender in "Bye Bye Birdie" at Clark Community College. Margie, who is a bartender, wonders if her son was typecast?

Also from the Joker: Ted Whetstone – "I intend to have as much fun in my adultery as I did in my infancy!"

Gary – "To have Dusty lose at least $20 at the 21 table." Obviously that makes my New Year's resolution to never lose more than $19.00!"

From the Cabaret come these resolutions: **ALEXIS** – "Stop dating cops, especially Libras."

DELILAH JONES – "Win the Mercedes at the Dunes."

DIEDRE RHODES – "Never to work for less than I'm worth (but she says there are some who think she's worthless!)"

Mako Ota – "To work toward human revolution and perfect life." (She's studying Buddhism).

Michelle – "I want to buy my own house."

TEDDY KING – "I want to buy more stock in Seagram's 7. If I had done it years ago, I would have been a self-made millionaire."

TURBAN – "I resolve not to let my current bird get away."

CHARLIE VESPIA – "Next year I'm not going to be so prejudiced. I'm going to hate everybody."

BOB MITCHELL – "I resolve to let my wife spend 150% of what I make, which will cut her way down."

Vegas Visitor

How Does a Man Get Into Burlesque?

1977 Burlesque has changed completely through the years. Where at one time, a burlesque show meant comedians and no strippers, now it is strippers and seldom comedians. So how, in this turnabout world, does a man get in to burlesque? I talked to **TURBAN** (pictured), who is the comedian, magician, and emcee at the Cabaret, a prominent burlesque club in Las Vegas, and asked him how he got his start.

Turban was doing a children's television show in Topeka, Kansas, when he moonlighted as a comic for a stag show at the Moose Club.

"I got there early and was setting up my show when the three exotics arrived. I explained to them that this was the only dressing room and I'd be out of their way in a couple of minutes. I turned back to my table and finished up and two minutes later, when I turned around, I was in a room with three naked ladies and I figured out this was the business to be in!"

Turban took his pictures and publicity to the T-Bone Club in Wichita, Kansas and was hired as the comic for the show.

"At that time, a comic did about 40 minutes and the stripper did 20 minutes making an hour show three times a night."

Turban warns would-be burlesque comics that burlesque is a hard business to get into. "There are few exotic clubs using comics any more. Comedy in burlesque is almost gone except for Las Vegas."

He also reveals that the hours are long in most clubs starting at nine or ten to as late as four or five in the morning. "And like Rodney Dangerfield says, 'You don't get no respect.' There is little of the glamour involved like there used to be unless you're a superstar. You're just grinding away like in any job."

Even with the long hours, Turban wouldn't trade places with anyone. "I'm just a ham," he admits. "I think that a great deal of the people who come to see a burlesque show DO come to see the comic and regardless of who they come to see, I'm going to make sure they remember me. They expect a show and they show their appreciation."

Asked where he gets the material for his show, Turban says, "I steal it! People tell me jokes a thousand times a week. I listen to everyone. You ad lib on stage, someone laughs and you keep it in the act."

Working with hundreds of strippers over the past 15 years, Turban has had the time to form opinions from a viewpoint few others are ever exposed to. "I think the majority of exotics are strong-willed business women. It takes a lot of guts to do what they do. Most of the girls are very professional people who put a lot of hard work and imagination in their shows."

Turban came to Las Vegas from Ft. Walton Beach, Florida after touring the rest of the southern states as the South's only top banana.

"I believe that Las Vegas is the entertainment answer. There are great audiences and the best performers in the world. Just like everyone else, I'm working for the big break. I think I could fit into any show on the Strip, adapting my comedy material to the show along with my magic. I've been waiting for Walter Kane to offer me a job but I guess I just haven't paid enough dues yet."

Vegas Visitor

1977 "Fevers Up" at the Landmark is a spicy show with lots of fun for everyone. I especially enjoyed the hilarious classic burlesque skits with J.C. Curtiss, **BILL FANNING**, Maggie Montgomery, and Bobbi Stamm.

Using a magic machine that will cause the diseases of a live person to go through it and into a store dummy, Bill Fanning as the doctor, is misled by Bobby Stamm as his secretary-nurse, into thinking her boyfriend, J.C. Curtiss, is the store dummy he is going to use with his new machine.

As each patient is hooked up to the machine, J.C. is left with a new affliction. First he itches, then he adds a stammering problem, then he assumes a "gay" personality, and then he caps it all off with the assumption of pregnancy, all of these simultaneously!

Pat Gill performs an exotic dance routine with two of the sexiest male dancers in Vegas. With their assistance, she deftly peels off a sophisticated black gown and then goes into some sexy nylon work on a prop framed in the word LOVE.

The Jerry Norman dancers were at their best and the black light number resembled a living pop art poster alive with glowing pinks, greens, and oranges dancing across the stage.

An outstanding number was an adagio routine to "All in Love Is Fair" sung by vocalist Celine Britt. The number was sensuously graceful and the dancers were so in tune with each other that their every movement spoke of love for one another. It was a very moving performance.

After the show, I talked with Bill Fanning about how he got his start in show business. As he told it, he played piano on the Gerry Johnson variety show in Dallas as a guest when the show's singer quit. Gerry offered Bill the job at $10 a day and he took it.

Breck Wall hired Gerry Johnson for his now infamous "Bottoms Up" and on her recommendation and without ever seeing him in person he also hired Bill.

"Three days before the show was to open the director quit the show. He said it was awful. Breck Wall told me I was terrible but just to do the best I could. I was dumb, I had a contract and I thought I had to do it so I stayed. We opened to rave reviews and that's the way it's been ever since."

"Breck Wall picked out all of my material. I've never known exactly what it is I do but he was able to see something in me and we've never missed. Left to myself I would pick out cutsie stuff that would die."

"In fact when I first auditioned my solo number "Somewhere Over The Rainbow," I never thought they'd buy it. But they did and it goes over great and I can't tell you why." (Note: because it's funny! It's a beautiful song, done well by Bill in a clown's outfit capped by a surprise punch line.)

Bill Fanning describes himself as a comedic actor. "I'm not a stand-up comedian. The closest I ever came to that was when I worked for four years with **CARME**." (Pictured below are Carme and Bill Fanning in 1973. Photo courtesy of Carme).

Right now, Bill is working on getting his first book published. Entitled *On With the Wind*, it is a collection of embarrassing stories having to do with a personal problem he has since been cured of!

This is your last chance to catch "Girls Ala Carte" at the Fremont Hotel.

Even if you've seen the show before, be sure to catch the new additions. Vanda is the new vocalist and does an especially good job on a Peggy Lee hit, "I'm A Woman."

Comedy is furnished by **JIMMY MATHEWS** (pictured) and Stan Stanley, two veteran burlesque comics.

Exotic performers include acrobatic dancer **JUDY MICHAELS**, sexy Francine, and the sensational star of the show **SUZETTE SUMMERS** (pictured).

Joining the all-star cast of exotics at the Cabaret are Penthouse cover girl **VALERIE RAY** and top-notch exotic **CASSANDRA LEE.**

Vegas Visitor

1977 What do those sweet little Gerber babies grow up to be? Why beautiful gorgeous exotics of course. I'm speaking specifically of Gerber baby model, **CHELSEA ALBREIGHT TIPTON** (pictured), brown eyes, 5'2", 36-25-34 and 107 pounds from Los Angeles.

Chelsea has grown up into a classic

burlesque artist complete with lace, black garters, nylons and some of the sexiest floor work in the business. She's appeared everywhere from Toronto to Tahiti, New York City to Honolulu. The only places she hasn't yet booked are Maine and Alaska!

Chelsea has also done a bit of modeling for *Playboy Magazine*, had a speaking role in "Pirate Girls" and performed in several television commercials.

I asked Chelsea about her future ambitions and I'm not sure how to interpret it but she says, "I want to be the worlds first "lay down" comic!"

Chelsea has a good sense of humor and enjoys kibitzing with her audience. She invites audience participation.

Side note: Seems Chelsea and I worked together several years ago at the Tender Trap in Phoenix, Arizona and before that at the Follies in New York City. Small world isn't it?

Vegas Visitor

1977 He's a comic who's worked with the likes of Ann Corio, Gypsy Rose Lee, and Georgia Southern. He's hosted his own late night talk show and starred in his own series. He's appeared with every big name in the business. He's a member of the infamous Frank Sinatra Clan. His childhood friends work with him in his highly successful and frequent appearances in Las Vegas at the Sahara's Congo Room. He is **JOEY BISHOP** (pictured).

Raised in South Philadelphia, Joey has been in show business since the age of 12 when he used to enter amateur contests winning them with his impersonations. He worked with the Minskey's and the Follies in 1938. You can still recognize traces of the old burlesque skits during the hilarious "interruption scenario" with the help of Gilbo Arcade as the bumbling waiter who also just happens to be a talented singer, and the deadpan bongo player Bill Heywood.

JOEY BISHOP

Playing still further with the scene are the fabulous Agostinos, an acrobatic adagio act who has also worked in burlesque. As Frank Agostino ("Clark Kent in disguise") hooks his feet under the straps of his famous Roman chair and bends over the back of the chair to balance his lovely partner Denise on his hands in preparation for lifting her straight up in the air from the floor, Joey is reminded from Denise's back view that he needs some fresh buns when he goes shopping!

As Joey prepares to do a number on his mandolin accompanied by Bill Heywood on the bongos, Gilbo Arcade, as a waiter who wants his big break, interrupts him. Gilbo wants to sing and Joey being generous allows him the floor, which Gilbo takes, completely blocking out the audience's view of

Joey. So Joey, in order to gain attention, leaves the stage briefly and returns in HIS waiter's jacket complete with tray.

Adapting much of his material specifically to the Las Vegas scene, Joey tells you how to drive a dedicated slot machine player crazy. "Wait until he's been playing an hour or so and has given up. Then walk up to the machine with your roll of quarters, put one quarter in the slot and fling the rest in the tray. Guaranteed to leave the previous player muttering the unprintable."

Joey vows that no one in Las Vegas sleeps. "They all take walking naps." He further comments on overhearing conversations about the weather in the summertime. "It's so nice here, 120 degrees but there's no humidity. Hot is hot!"

He also apologizes for any empty

seats, "It's due to all the icy roads."

Joey's deadpan easy-going delivery effectively draws laughs with every line. He even coaches the audience so they will know when to laugh and applaud. "Since we don't have applause signs like they do in the television studios, I'll just raise up on one foot at the punch line. Then he proceeds to test the audience with the corniest joke he can tell and it works.

By the end of the show, Joey has earned a standing ovation for the show he wrote and put together.

Gilbo Arcade, Joey's right hand man on and off the stage, was brought out of show business retirement and the real estate business to join Joey three years ago. The Agostinos have worked with Joey many times in the 21 years they've been married. And most amazing of all, they all grew up together in South Philadelphia. Now how's that for keeping up with old friends?

Vegas Visitor

1977 That sexy redhead who just opened at the Fremont in "Girls A La Carte" is vivacious, acrobatic exotic, **JUDY MICHAELS** (pictured).

A long time Las Vegas resident, Judy grew up in show business, singing, acting and dancing her way through such movies and shows as "Music Man," "Thunder In The Sun," "Wonderful World of Color," "Real McCoy's," "Bachelor Father," and dozens of others. She appeared weekly in the "Donald O'Connor Show," a Los Angeles based variety television show, for three years and went on the road with it for two more years. It was this show that finally brought her to Las Vegas at the age of 17 for her first appearance at the Sahara.

Since then, Judy has danced in numerous production shows in Las Vegas, as well as choreographing some of them and making the costumes. Judy learned how to sew from her mother who works in the wardrobe department at MGM.

Judy is also an accomplished piano player and is presently putting together a country western lounge show featuring her talents as a vocalist and dancer along with some other surprises.

Another beautiful redheaded exotic, **PATTY WRIGHT** (pictured), billed as "The Only Tap Dancing Exotic," opened at the Cabaret with over $7000 in wardrobe made especially for her first Las Vegas appearance by Hedy Jo Starr, the Bob Mackie of the burlesque world.

Featuring six completely different shows, Patty has something for everyone. Red-blooded Americans will especially enjoy her "Tribute to America" featuring, believe it or not, our National Anthem as well as all of the armed service anthems.

Patty also has a spider show complete with spider web, a florescent butterfly show and a special show featuring her tap dancing talents to Broadway hits, like "Give My Regards to Broadway." Patty is an exciting addition to the Cabaret line-up of exotic beauties.

Brandy Wine is now teasing the patrons of the Sun Dancer along with **DELILAH DANTE** and **JAN FON-TAINE**.

Vegas Visitor

January 6, 1978   The triple –X-rated master of mirth and magic, **PROFESSOR TURBAN**, departs Las Vegas for an engagement at the Embers in Anchorage, Alaska. Bon voyage and brrr!

ARTIE BROOKS, comedy star of the Palomino, tells me that he is putting out an album of his material. "It will be on a 23 RPM record so people can get the jokes the first time around."

Artie brought his mother Marjorie to Las Vegas recently to live with him. One night she called the club asking for Artie. "Tell him it's just a small emergency, not a big one, a small one," she told **BARBIE DOLL**.

A quick check of the club revealed that Artie had gone down the street to get something to eat and someone was sent after him. Barbie got on the phone to Artie's mother and told her that he should be back in a few minutes and could he call her?

Joni Jansen continues to captivate the audiences at the Jolly Trolley.

Rumor has it that the Tender Trap is going burlesque this month! Many of the jazz fans will be disappointed but apparently girl watchers out number them.

There's plenty of go-go action at the Gilded Cage in North Las Vegas. Between dance sets the girls also serve the lucky customers their favorite drinks and there's no cover charge or minimum.

Don't forget the Palomino Club open from 2PM with more exotics than you can count on all your fingers and toes and one of the funniest comics in town, **BOB MITCHELL**.

"Well, I guess that's alright," said Artie's mother, sounding just a bit worried. "Three minutes. Well, tell him the apartments full of smoke!"

Now that's consideration! She didn't want to bother Artie over anything small! Actually the apartment was full of smoke from the fireplace. Nothing serious after all. But what a mother he has.

GINA BON BON is back at the Cabaret from her recent road tour and plans to stay in Las Vegas for a while. Catch her scintillating performance in the daytime show.

"Auditions being held for waiters and waitresses." That's right, auditions to work at Tony's Penthouse on Vegas Valley Drive. You must be able to sing.

Accompanied by Ronnie Trent on organ, I had the pleasure of hearing club owner Tony Luciano crooning "Old Devil Moon" and "On A Clear Day." His performance was followed by the introduction of his newest waitress, lovely blonde Amber, who put her heart in the classical "Summertime" from Porgy and Bess and the beautiful Burt Bacharach's "Look of Love."

In addition to the all-entertaining crew, the Penthouse is offering disco sounds between sets, baskets of delicious food and special house drinks including something called Brazilian Caipirinia "made just like they drink it in Rio." It's a blend of vodka, sugar, limes, and soda. For tequila lovers there is the Cactus Nut, which is tequila and amaretto over ice.

Every Thursday night is Gong Night with weekly prize winners competing each month for a weeks paid contract at the Penthouse and those winners vie at the years end for a weeks all-expense paid vacation to the Penthouse's sister club in San Paulo, Brazil.

One of Las Vegas' finest magicians **DARWIN** presents a "Night of Magic" each Wednesday night in Pat's Chinese Kitchen's Dragon Lounge. The show features Darwin and his nude illusions. And at midnight you can see the greatest magicians in the world as they gather to perform for each other and interested spectators.

Vegas Visitor

January 13, 1978 A former exotic school dance instructor, **K.C. LAYNE** (pictured), recently opened at the Cabaret. Originally from Kansas City, where she began her career as a dancer, K.C. eventually settled in Nashville, Tennessee performing in several shows and choreographing others. With another dancer, she operated a school for exotic dancers and also taught housewives routines to spice up their marital lives. After a vacation in Las Vegas, K.C. went back to Nashville and closed up shop for a permanent move and what she expects to be "a great new experience" in our exciting city.

Also back at the Cabaret, after another road tour, is the saucy "Love Potion Candy Girl," **GINA BON BON**. She sent me an example of her road popularity in a newspaper clipping from San Antonio, where she was the front-page headline: "Bon Bon Is Back!"

After a successful engagement at Skulls Rainbow in Nashville, lithe and lovely **VELVET ODESSEY** is back in the night time show at the Palomino.

Also returning to the Palomino from an engagement at the Golden Banana in Boston is fiery black haired beauty **SALUMBA**. She loved the club there but she said the winter weather was miserable.

ARTIE BROOKS, comedy star at the Palomino, introduced me to his ex-wife's beautiful daughter 13-year old Grace Morely. A model since the age of five, Grace has appeared as centerfold for Parker Brothers Games, modeled for Carter's sleepwear, appeared in the "Crazy Form Girl" a national syndication and has had many other modeling assignments.

Grace is an accomplished dancer and has entertained at theater groups and charity functions. She also loves tennis, swimming, gymnastics, golf, volleyball and track. She is already a member of AFTRA and SAG.

Grace recently left Massachusetts and intends to make her home in Las Vegas where she can continue pursuing her career in acting and modeling. Good luck!

Vegas Visitor

February 17, 1978 The multi-talented **ANGEL CARTER** (pictured), now appearing at the Cabaret Burlesque Palace, started singing and dancing when she was just a baby in her native Samoa.

Later she moved to Hollywood, California where she continued her dancing career and added legitimate modeling and several appearances in films and television to her resume.

ANGEL CARTER

Angel has toured the country and even took a male dance partner to Tokyo and to Canada in a special dance review of her own. In fact, during one of her tours, she worked with me at the Tender Trap in Phoenix, Arizona.

At 5'6" tall, the 38½D-24-36 brunette beauty was also one of Barry Ashton's showgirls. She explains, "Dancing is in my blood."

Angel contemplates a permanent move to Las Vegas, "if everything works out." She especially enjoys working at the Cabaret. "It's a beautiful club with beautiful girls and a great boss."

Eventually she'd like to put her own

band together and says that she prefers country western and also enjoys light rock, oldies but goodies, and the blues.

Angel is studying a film script right now but she's too superstitious to let the name out!

The "Olde Tyme Burlesque" review at the Maxim starring **ANN MARIE**, 67-25-36, and top banana **BOB MITCHELL** is doing turn-away business! Those of us in the cast would like to thank all our friends for coming to see us. And thanks to the Maxim Hotel management for making us feel so welcome.

Vegas Visitor

March 3, 1978   The cast and crew of "Girls A Poppin" at the Cabaret Burlesque Palace recently bid a reluctant farewell to manager **TEX MARSHAL** (pictured), who is returning to the entertainment world as a country singer.

Tex, one of the original members of the Bob Wills Texas Playboys, is well known around Las Vegas as he played

nearly every club in town at one time or another including the Silver Dollar (formerly the Saddle Club) where he was a mainline attraction over 15 years performing as Tex Marshall and the Texas Rodeo Ranchhands.

Tex is an important part of the history of Las Vegas and remembers when he used to ride a horse downtown to work! He had several television and radio shows in town and was an ardent supporter of civic and charitable projects.

Presently he is being considered to play the role of Tommy Duncan in the life story movie about Bob Wills. Tex considers it quite an honor as he backed up Tommy Duncan for several years. Tommy was most famous for his "San Antonio Rose" record, which has now sold over six million copies.

Tex was also a popular figure in much of the west appearing extensively in California, especially in Bakersfield. Tex had a radio show when he worked in Vallejo. One of his letters of commendation complained that Tex shouldn't be allowed to take vacations. "Without him" reads the commendation, "the music isn't the same."

Tex has a remarkable recall of country music lyrics. He can sing over six hours without repeating a song. One of his most requested numbers is "Danny Boy." He also knows such oldies as "Canadian Sunset," Ghost Riders In the Sky," "Cool Water," and "Streets of Laredo."

Tex has performed with many of the big country artists including Ferlin

Husky, Merle Travis, Marty Robbins, Buck Owens, and Hank Snow.

Asked for his own favorite artist in country music, Tex says, "If I had to pick out one singer across the times, it would have to be Marty Robbins." He also enjoys the sounds of Eddy Arnold, Johnny Horton, Jim Reeves, and Mel Tillis.

Fans eagerly await the return of Tex to country music and he expects to be back on the bandstand again in just a few weeks.

Vegas Visitor

March 10, 1978 The "Rare 'N Bare" show at the Royal Las Vegas, starring comic-ventriloquist **LOU DUPONT** (pictured), has an almost entirely new cast than when I last saw the show a couple of months ago. The only remaining member, besides Lou, is the lovely **NICOLE** still doing a variety of entertaining exotic routines including her newest with an Indian theme using selections such as "Cherokee Nation," "Witchy Woman," and "Apache," and climaxing with the production of a beautiful white dove. Following Nicole is Deva, a pretty brunette who performs an exhilarating, fast-paced jazz routine.

Next is a familiar face to many Vegas burlesque buffs, the buxom blonde beauty **LIBERTY WEST**. The highlight of her sexy routine is a beautiful spiraling chiffon negligee routine to "Happy Days are Here Again." It is some of the best cape work I've seen.

Rounding out the show is dark-haired beauty Heather Minsky, one of burlesque's top exotic attractions, gowned in an elegant silver cape with turkey boa trim over a black sequin skin-tight dress. She performs the old time strip, where the teasing is an art, as she

skillfully peels out of her wardrobe to display a Playboy centerfold body.

The newest burlesque show in Vegas is at the Joker Club featuring the lovely **TERI STARR** and including a full cast of exotic beauties with emceeing by redhead beauty **JUDY MICHAELS**. It is a continuous show from 9PM to 2AM.

Returning to the Cabaret is comic-magician **TURBAN** after his brief stay in Anchorage, Alaska. Seems he had to come back to Vegas to thaw out. He says the Eskimos really get wild up there!

Opening March 13 at the Cabaret is Vincene "Goddess of Love" and one of the stars of the Russ Meyers film "Vixen." Vincene is a tall, beautiful redhead who does a dynamite job on stage. I had the pleasure of working with her in Ft. Walton Beach, Florida and she never failed to please an audience.

PATTY WRIGHT is booked to open in a burlesque review in Mexico City and then on to Acapulco.

PAULETTE PARKER (P.J.) has recovered from her knee injury and recently opened at the Palomino. She is wowing the lucky patrons with her unbelievable dancing skills. Paulette is from a burlesque family and has grown up on the burlesque circuit in the most delightfully pleasing way!

"Olde Tyme Burlesque" at the Maxim is going strong. Lots of celebrities have been dropping in to see this dynamite show including June Allyson, Jack Kelly, the Argentina Gauchos, Chuck Eastwood, Skull Shullman, Tony Curtis, and Rodney Dangerfield. Word is out that this is the hit of the year! Thank you everyone!

Vegas Visitor

March 23, 1978 There's lots of action in Las Vegas as some of the country's top exotics tread the runways in our fabulous burlesque palaces.

Combining brains and beauty is the circle-turner herself, the flying exotic **JAN FONTAINE**. Jan can make you dizzy as she whirls around the stage, flashing her warm smile, rocking to a bit of disco and having even more fun if the songs include anything about airplanes! Jan is a licensed pilot whose second favorite maneuver in the sky is to locate out of the way landing strips. You can just guess what her FAVORITE maneuver is by her bumper sticker "pilots do it in the air!"

Right now you can catch Jan at the Joker Club in North Las Vegas. She's sure to take you on a trip you won't forget.

Among the lovely ladies at the Palomino Club is the blonde beauty **SNOWY SINCLAIRE**. Avid girl watchers will recognize Snowy from the many times she's appeared in *Playboy Magazine*.

Another winner at the Palomino is **BARBI DOLL**. Barbi adds a large helping of comedy to her show with dozens of ad-libs. She also uses a long black whip to keep her court in order! Things do get rowdy when Barbi struts her stuff!

The Cabaret has an all day and all night line-up of more than 15 girls so there is bound to be the girl of your dreams somewhere in the show. For many, this girl is the talented **TRACY SUMMERS** whose face and form grace many of the billboards about town.

Tracy is known for her bubbling stage personality as well as a variety of show ideas including the portrayal of a gypsy, a lady of the evening, and a person from outer space, a disco queen, and dozens of others. Tracy delivers her version of the sensuous lady in all of her shows.

At the Crazy Horse you'll enjoy Cimmaron, who can bend her beautiful body into some very backbreaking positions. You'll fall in love with her long red hair and the twinkle in her green eyes as she takes you home to meet Grandma in her "Little Red Riding Hood Show." Any wolves out there?

And for lots of laughs as well as exotic talent, you'll love **BOB MITCHELL** and **CHARLIE VESPIA** in "Olde Tyme Burlesque at the Maxim Hotel. Along with hilarious baggy pants skits, you'll enjoy the dancing talents of **ANGELIQUE PETTYJOHN** and my magic with assistant **BRANDY DURAN** who also provides the feminine touch to the comedy portion of the show.

Burlesque fans rejoice for you are in Las Vegas!

Vegas Visitor

March 31, 1978   One of the first people visiting magicians make a point of meeting is **GARY DARWIN** (pictured). A Las Vegas resident for more than 24 years, he teaches magic, performs professionally, and holds the most talked about magic meetings in the nation at Pat's Chinese Kitchen every Wednesday starting at midnight. It is attended by some of the worlds leading professionals, including Siegfried and Roy, Grippo, Professor Turban, Le Ruse, Ricco, Johnny Paul, Tomsoni, and Berri Lee. Amateur magicians can get advice from the best. Magic lovers can see magic performed by magicians in an informal, friendly setting.

On Wednesday afternoons at 4PM, Darwin holds a special meeting primarily for aspiring young magicians at Fabulous Magic Company. In addition to demonstrating various effects offered for sale at the shop, Darwin helps the youngsters with basic magic including slight of hand, coin moves, and stage presence as well as the more sophisticated principles of the large illusions and even mystifying mind reading.

The children have a chance to perform for each other on a special stage in the shop. In fact, if you are looking for a special effect, one of the young amateurs can probably demonstrate it for you.

Darwin got his love for magic when he was a child being entertained by his grandfather, an avid amateur magician. His grandfather, Darwin recalls, "was constantly pulling out fifty cent pieces from my ear and then he'd give them to me. But he'd never show me how to do any magic. You can imagine how that affected a six year old. He sparked an interest in me that continues today."

Besides entertaining at a multitude of charitable events, Darwin has appeared professionally at Caesars Palace, The Mint, Stardust, Flamingo, Hacienda, Silverbird, and Desert Inn.

He has also lectured the past five years at UNLV on magic as well as tutored private classes.

Darwin's home is actually a magic showcase. He has hundreds of books on magic and virtually every magic effect in existence, many one of a kind. "Professionals often drop by and borrow a particular effect from me," admits Darwin. He also has a dove aviary in his back yard.

Darwin has invented over 200 original effects himself. He is now in the process of publishing a book on the history of the hundred greatest magicians under the sponsorship of Siegfried.

Presently, Darwin is working on a show in which he hopes to incorporate the art of burlesque, something all burlesque and magic fans will be looking forward to.

Vegas Visitor

April 7, 1978 Want to get started in show business but don't know quite how to go about it? Do you want to be a comic, a belly dancer, an actor, a magician, or an exotic dancer and wish you could learn the inside story from a professional?

Now there is a new school offering just that kind of training called Studio for the Performing Arts run by veteran entrepreneur-producer Harry Van Valin (over 35 years experience in nightclubs and every phase of entertainment). All of the instructors are professionals presently appearing in Las Vegas.

The studio, located in the Commercial Center, is a full service studio. It is large and well equipped including a full size stage with a runway, mirrors to check your work, lighting and a professional sound system. There are even some exercycles to limber you up before class!

The day I visited, the studio exotic-instructor **LOVEY GOLDMINE** was in the middle of choreographing a full burlesque routine for a cute little blonde from the Jolly Trolley named Cindy. Lovey explained the routine they were working on was from the Broadway Play "Annie" and Cindy was working on mime. "She's a fantastic dancer," says Lovey, who should know since she was the star of the revue at Le Crazy Horse in Paris, France and is currently appearing at the Cabaret. "What she needs is a routine that suits her personality and a few sexy moves that are unique to burlesque. I'm also choreographing a show for her where she will just walk and peel seductively. Aside from that, we're concentrating on more exaggerated moves for the bigger stages."

Says Harry of his exotic instructor, "I've been in this business a long time and worked with hundreds of girls and I think Lovey is the best dancer-exotic I've ever seen and she's an excellent teacher. We're very lucky to have her.

Other instructors at the school will include the beautiful Sumi, star of the Holiday Casino, who will be teaching belly dancing. The Palomino's zany comic **ARTIE BROOKS** will instruct stand-up comedy. Master illusionist and magician comic **PROFESSOR TURBAN** of the Cabaret will introduce students to the world of magic. Ion De Hondol, internationally renowned actor-director, formerly an associate with the American Academy of Dramatic Arts, will conduct drama classes.

A short time ago I did an article on Sahara's Talent Showcase mentioning the Porters, Phil age 11 and Tina age 9, and how they were "discovered" and signed to appear with Totie Fields in her recent engagement at the Sahara. I was fortunate enough to have a chance to catch the talented youngsters and to hear Totie announce that she intended to take the duo with her on the rest of her road tour. So all you hopefuls head for the Sahara Casbar for auditions Monday at 1PM with performances from 9PM and maybe you'll be the next success story!

Vegas Visitor

April 1978   Featured exotic in Rocky Sennes "Wild World of Burlesque '78" at the Holiday Casino is **MISS SANDY O'HARA** (pictured), "The Improper Bostonian." This engagement marks Sandy's first appearance since she headlined "Love of Sex" at the Hacienda in 1974. She was also featured in Barry Ashton's "Wonderful World of Burlesque" at the Silver Slipper and in "Minsky's Follies" at the Aladdin.

At the Holiday, Miss O'Hara gives strip tease a touch of the elegance and class that has been identified with some of the great ladies in burlesque such as Gypsy Rose Lee, Sally Rand, and Tempest Storm. She is every inch an elegant and classy lady, lending to her show almost a touch of royalty as she gracefully peels off her Paris gowns and adds a bit of spice when she wiggles seductively to the lucky patrons sitting up front.

When Sandy finishes her strip show, she dons her nursing uniform to play talking lady to top banana Claude Mathis with **DEXTER MAITLAND** in the classic burlesque scene: "The Transformer," thus enabling the audience to further view her talents as an accomplished comedic actress.

Sandy has been happily married to producer David Hanson for eleven years and between appearances with Ann Corio and some nightclub bookings, she stars in her husband's productions. These have included "The Best of Burlesque," "Grin and Bare It," and most recently "Remember Ol' Scollay Square" which toured the prestigious Chateau de Ville Dinner Theaters throughout New England.

SANDY O'HARA

Appearing with Sandy at the Holiday are the marvelous Walkers, one sister and two brothers who, sing and impersonate their way through such personalities as Johnny Cash, Elvis Presley, Sonny & Cher, but best of all a hilarious and almost true to life Dolly Parton. A harmonica solo by one of the brothers is definitely the highlight of their show and is worth seeing in itself.

I've always enjoyed Jay Nemeth and Nicky the loveable little pooch who lives in a suitcase! I last saw Jay at the Hacienda and he is a big favorite with Las Vegas producers. Everyone enjoys his brand of comedy and I think they forget that Nicky isn't a real dog.

As always, the Betty Francisco Dancers add the rounded out touches of a full floorshow with their can can number, the banjo routine and even a silhouetted strip tease by all six of the girls.

In addition to representing some of the finest exotics in the country, the **JESS MACK AGENCY** also represents a number of legitimate acts and is a representative for the Screen Actors Guild. One of their current clients is handsome Michael Allyn who has been cast in the role of Riff for the Theatre Arts Society, Inc. production of "West Side Story." The show opened April 13 at the Reed Whipple Cultural Arts Center and continues with ten performances through the 29th.

Get well wishes go out to Herbie Fay, well known for his performances in

Phil Silvers "Sergeant Bilko Show" and to Ronnie Rogich, box office girl for the Maxim's "Olde Tyme Burlesque Show."

Special laurels to Maxim's comedy star, **BOB MITCHELL,** who helped save a youngster in a runaway car accident by giving him artificial respiration. Bob was too modest to stick around for his thank-you!

Vegas Visitor

April 28, 1978 "Olde Tyme Burlesque" is still going strong at the Maxim with new show times of 8, 10, and 12 and a special 2 a.m. show on Friday and Saturday along with a new bargain show price of $7.50. Featured in the show are the acrobatic dancing talents of **TRIANA ZZON** as well as yours truly with magic-burlesque style and the uproarious antics of Top Banana **BOB MITCHELL, and** zany **CHAR-LIE VESPIA** (pictured) along with beautiful **CHRISTINE DARLING.** This is one show where comedy is definitely the highlight and "seller." There are never two shows in a row exactly alike due to the quick ad-libbing by the cast in the infamous old time burlesque scenes. Bob will amaze you when you see him play THREE horns at the same time.

More laughter and magic is provided at the Cabaret by **TURBAN. He manages to weave his own brand of X-rated mirth and magic throughout the night. A welcome back goes to redheaded LOVEY GOLDMINE as** she brings to the Cabaret stage some new and entertaining routines.

Adding the charm of an Aztec prin-cess at the Palomino is the exquisitely beautiful **SALUMBA** (pictured). In addition to some of the most elegant wardrobe in the business, Salumba carries herself with an unequaled grace punctuating her show with various spicy ad libs in her beautiful Spanish accent. She could easily be another Charo!

PATRICK, "The All American Stripper," writes from Del Webb's Sahara Tahoe to say all is going well. He enclosed a review of his show, which aptly describes Patrick as "looking like a grandiose, glittery Gene Kelly in moves, but rapidly changing to a male version of Lili St. Cyr in intent." The show is called "Wow '78" and any of you fortunate enough to have caught him here at Le Café know just what that means. I am looking forward to seeing him back again in Vegas. Special note to Patrick: Your one time partner Triana would like to know why you don't write her!

Vegas Visitor

May 5, 1978 Burlesque buffs will enjoy an evening of fine exotic entertainment at the Joker Club in North Las Vegas. Headlining the continuous show is **TERI STARR** and the cast includes Cherry, **K.C. LAYNE** and April, with **JUDY MICHAELS** as mistress if ceremonies.

Teri and K.C. have been going to poker school and K.C. has already landed a job as a poker dealer at a major hotel. You can catch Teri practicing on the 21 tables at the Joker Club between shows!

BARBIE DOLL, who appears nightly at the Palomino, recently entered a talent contest at the 101 Club between shows. She wasn't able to stay for the judging but she did receive a letter from Encore Records applauding her talents as a country singer and expressing interest in some future recording work. Barbie has already toured with the Bobby Durham Show as featured female vocalist and she sang with Waylon Jennings too!

"Flame of the Jet Set" **SUSI MID-NITE** (pictured), also appearing at the Palomino, had some special friends with her as she attended Peter Marshal's recent appearance with Buddy Hackett at the Sahara. Monty Hall and one of the associate producers of the Mike Douglas show were her escorts. Susi, who is a big fan of Peter Marshall, told me she had never seen Buddy Hackett perform before and that he was hilarious. "He kept me in stitches the whole show, and that's hard to do when you've seen as many comics as I have. He was the funniest I've ever heard."

Former exotic Electra Powers (Lela) is now cocktailing at Caesars Palace. The burlesque world loses quite a talent but I'm sure Caesars' patrons will benefit.

The afternoon show at the Cabaret is going great thanks to an all-star line-up including the talents of exotic-actress **ANGEL CARTER**. Angel has been in lots of television and movie scenes and she is also a fine country singer.

Vegas Visitor

May 12, 1978   One of the latest additions to the all-star line-up of exotics at the world famous Palomino Club in North Las Vegas is "The Toast of San Francisco," lovely auburn haired **CHAMPAGNE** (pictured).

Coming to Las Vegas from the Golden Banana, near Boston, where she was a featured dancer over eight months, Champagne has an elegant wardrobe and a variety of shows including a 50s number, a tuxedo number (Fred Astaire style) as well as the elegant "Toast of San Francisco" show.

Her 50's show has a bit of "history in the making" story behind it. Seems Massachusetts's officials weren't too pleased about having nude dancers so they took the Golden Banana to court. The Golden Banana had a videotape of Champagne's performance as part of their evidence. Although they lost the first round, they later won their case on

appeal.

Champagne is especially determined to create an aura of class when she performs. "My 50s show is one of the cleanest and at the same time most entertaining shows I do. It won't offend anybody."

Although Champagne has been an exotic for less than two years, she's been dancing all her life. "My mother was a chorus line dancer for Fred Waring. Even when I walked, she wanted it perfect. I started dance lessons at three years old and between her and my teachers, I had lessons in tap, ballet, jazz, ballroom dancing, even square dancing."

But what Champagne excelled at was gymnastics. For ten years she participated in vaulting and floor exercise with the balance beam being her specialty. Just as she was preparing for the 1968 Olympic tryouts, she injured herself doing a cartwheel on the balance beam, terminating what may have been a promising career as an athlete.

Champagne began her career in show business as a go-go dancer at the Playgirl in Concord, California. She went on from there to dance in Seattle and Denver, eventually returning to California and her first job as an exotic at the Sutter Street Theatre in San Francisco where she was held over six months.

Besides dancing, Champagne has tried a bit of modeling and made some commercials for Doral Records. She was awarded a couple of titles while she was at the Golden Banana including "Miss Vernon Liquors" and "Miss General Electric." The title she is most proud of is that of "Miss 99 Club" which she earned by lending her talents to help raise $5000 for the Cancer Foundation of the Children's Hospital.

Champagne plans to continue entertaining in the burlesque world and she says she'd like to get more into comedy.

Vegas Visitor

May 17, 1978   Singer, dancer, actress **ANGEL CARTER**, now appearing at the Cabaret Burlesque Palace, puts on one of the most provocative and energetic shows in burlesque. This talented lady knows how to dance and with extraordinary measurements of 38½D-24-36, the 5'6" brunette beauty has no trouble keeping her audiences attention. Angel has also been cast as an extra in Vega$!

PATTY WRIGHT is now appearing with **STEVE ROSSI** in "Burlesque '79" at the Holiday International

Whatever she decides, she is a lady well endowed and most certainly gifted with the talent and ambition to go far.

downtown. She's really excited about working in the all-new showroom.

SHERRY SHANE (pictured) at the Joker Club has put together a dynamite act as a spider! Her show includes some of Vincent Price's dialogue and some creative musical selections including "Welcome To My Nightmare." She has a most original costume with a cape of rhinestone spider-like black bands and a dress that kind of weaves its way around her body. Sherry was one of the former amateurs from the Palomino Club.

Every now and then burlesque performers get together and celebrate weddings and other important events. Pictured below are **LOVEY GOLDMINE, ALEXIS, DUSTY SUMMERS, ANGELIQUE PETTYJOHN** and **JAN FONTAINE** (in front).

Note: This was my wedding reception and was the best part of a VERY short Marriage!

Pictured below is Dusty Summers and Paul Perry (1978).

Vegas Visitor

May 26, 1978 **SONSEAHRAY** (pictured) at 23 years old has already accumulated more experience in the world of burlesque than most girls have at the age of 30. Her secret? She started at the unbelievable age of 15 years when she ran away from an achievement center in Texas, making it to Houston where, as she sat in a coffee shop pouring over the want ads, she spotted one for topless dancers. She knew a job was mandatory if she didn't want to get caught so she auditioned and got her first job at the Rhembrant Paint Factory where she stayed for six months.

From there she went to Los Angeles and got a job at the Classic Cat with the aid of some fake I.D. and a kind-hearted owner who, although he looked the other way at a girl who was obviously under age, also looked out for her welfare while she worked for him.

"The people there were like a family to me," relates Sonseahray. "They made sure I didn't run with the wrong crowd and Alan (the owner) was quick to let me know when I made a mistake."

Sonseahray stayed at the Classic Cat a year and a half before she joined the Ray Valerie Review and went to Anchorage, Alaska. After only two weeks, the members of the band were deported for not having proper immigration visas and Sonseahray was stranded in Anchorage until she found a job go-go dancing.

Next came the Ginger Court Review back in Los Angeles, where in addition to dancing, Sonseahray assisted Ginger as part of a hypnotist act. The show traveled from Los Angeles to Illinois and Denver and then Sonseahray returned to the Classic Cat where she was part of a love team act.

From the Classic Cat, she came to Las Vegas and worked for **PAUL PERRY** at the Palomino and then went on a national tour during which she won the titles of "Miss Nude Galaxy" and "Miss Nude Entertainment" at the Ponderosa Sun Club in Roselawn, Indiana.

Sonseahray is Irish and Indian and her show name is an Apache name meaning "star that shines in the morning." Born in Browning, Montana, she was raised in Illinois. "All over Illinois," she explains.

If you want to see the lovely performances of the very exotic Sonseahray, make a trip to the Palomino during the daytime show, which starts at 2PM. Sonseahray is contemplating a retirement from burlesque in order to go back to school to be a medical technician so this may be your last chance. Don't miss it!

Vegas Visitor

June 2, 1978 The jazziest exotic in town is now performing at the Cabaret Burlesque Palace in the person of **P.J. PARKER**. You will also recognize P.J.'s name as one of the prominent columnists about town. The New Orleans-Chicago type jazz rendition, complete with expert pantomime and perfectly timed and executed moves, is just one of the many shows by this amazing acrobatic exotic.

A member of a burlesque family including sister, Amber Lynn, mother, comedienne Ava Leigh and father, comic Gene Graham, P, J.'s been in burlesque since she was 13. When the regular girls in her mothers carnival show demanded a raise she couldn't afford, P.J. was the only member of the family left. She became Velvet Knight because she had dark hair. Later the girls bleached her hair with a combination of peroxide, ammonia, and Lux. From that unlikely mixture was born blonde exotic Paulette Powers now Paulette Parker.

P.J. has just returned to Vegas after a cross-country tour including Florida and much of the Midwest, hitting some of the top nightclubs such as Surfside Seven in Ft. Walton Beach, Florida, Club Juana in Orlando, Florida and Skull's Rainbow Room in Nashville.

It was just about a year ago that I last wrote on P.J. and she was about to celebrate her wedding anniversary. This July 28, it will be four years. Congratulations!

More congratulations go out to **CHARLIE VESPIA** and his wife on the birth of their EIGHTH child Cynthia.

Charlie is one of the comedy stars of "Olde Tyme Burlesque" at the Maxim Hotel.

GEORGETTE DANTE, former star at the Royal Las Vegas, returned this week for a well-earned vacation. She's been touring as the star of the Ann Corio show as well as being featured in a number of Sheraton Hotels. From here she goes to warm up Alaska and then off for a tour of Asia and Europe.

During a recent meeting of Gary Darwin's Magic Club at Pat's Chinese Kitchen, Judy Wolfe, publicity writer, made her first stage appearance as a magician. She presented a well-executed rope trick. Darwin used my guest **TRIANNA ZZON** to perform the appearing and disappearing sponge balls and also a bit of business where he produced her bra!

Had the pleasure of meeting Siegfried & Roy, Daniel Cross, Earl Chaney, and many others whose names are synonymous with professional magicians in Las Vegas. The meetings are held every Wednesday night from midnight on and all magicians and interested guests are welcome.

Vegas Visitor

June 1978 The newest show on the Strip is "Fantasy Follies" at the Jolly Trolley, starring exotics **SUZETTE SUMMERS, ROBIN-O,** and **CASSANDRA LEE** (pictured). Presenting three completely different shows nightly except Monday, "Fantasy Follies" takes you on a "trip into the fantasies of your mind, past present and future." I arrived just in time for the future.

The future is interpreted as space and more precisely "Star Wars" and there are some excellent musical selections setting the tone.

The show opens with Robin-O and Cassandra Lee in all white costumes resembling Eskimos from the moon and they frolic around the stage investigating the strange aliens in the audience. Next comes the entrance of Darth Vader aka Suzette Summers as a robot wearing a costume made of metal riveting and a black cape she expertly and ominously twirls around her body. She proceeds to strip as provocatively as she is known for doing, each move a tease.

As Suzette winds up her strip, Robin-O enters the stage in a cute red wraparound shorty with fringe and rhinestones set off with a wide gold belt and carrying with her a whip to scare away the evil Darth Vader. It is often difficult for two girls to execute movements on stage with one mostly undressed without coming off lesbian but Suzette and Robin have managed to achieve just the right amount of parrying with the whip before Suzette exits so Robin can command the stage.

Robin does what I call a go-go type show in that she moves fast and furiously, but she does manage to wind down towards the end with some nice sexy moves. She has lots of sex appeal too with a million dollar body. Very few girls could top her in that category.

Next up is the good guy Cassandra Lee in a costume of clear vinyl and lots of silver lame. She executes a number with a green neon sword perfectly.

And there you have it: future "Fantasy Follies." It is a quick-paced show cleverly held together with the right music, the right costumes and the right girls. The few weak spots were mostly technical. The opening music was too long and the audience had to sit in complete darkness through it. Some light work would have kept the voices around me from asking "When's the show going to start?" The girls are working hard on the show and sometimes it shows when it appears that they are trying to put too much action in the show and not enough into audience play.

SUZETTE SUMMERS, ROBIN-O and CASSANDRA LEE

However, the show is well worth seeing, all three girls are beautiful and highly professional with credits reading like the who's who of burlesque. Suzette has starred at the Palomino, Joker Club, Fremont, and Holiday Casino. Robin and Cassandra have both starred at the Royal Las Vegas. Cassandra also starred at the Silver Slipper. Additionally all three girls work frequently in Minksy's and Barry Ashton's reviews.

Vegas Visitor

June 16, 1978 The world-famous Palomino Club is packing them in in North Las Vegas with their nude amateur dance contest held nightly, emceed by funnyman **ARTIE BROOKS**, as well as an all-star cast of beautiful exotics starting at 2PM and running continuously until 4:30 in the morning.

Artie gets girls up out of the audience to compete against each other for big cash prizes. When the amateurs take a break, the professionals put on a complete show featuring such beauties as **SUSI MIDNIGHT,** Valentina, **BARBI DOLL,** and **K.C. LAYNE.**

Susi told me she plans to spend her only night off winging it to Palm Springs for a special appearance of the Trench Rats (Veterans). She'll be joined on the trip by exotic Cherry from the Cabaret.

I hear the Joker Club is undergoing some changes in order to put in a special buffet. I know the cook personally and believe me it has to be good eating.

Glad to see **CIMMARON** back at the Royal Las Vegas. This beautiful red headed acrobatic is also a drama major at UNLV.

Saw Tiffany Holiday doing her thing at the Jolly Trolley. After a terrible car accident, it is really great to see Tiffany back in action and looking good.

I got a chance to see Glen Smith and Billy Kay at the Frontier Winner's Circle Lounge. They provide great entertainment and you can satisfy that keno urge at the same time. Be sure and request "McArthur Park" from Glen and the baseball routine from Billy Kay.

Terry Richards brings back the sound of jazz to the MGM lounge for two weeks. Singer Tom Christi will follow Terry.

PROFESSSOR TURBAN, comic-magician is opening at the Conover Hotel in Miami Beach along with singer **JEANNE THOMAS** in "Girls Ala Carte" produced by Jack LaMansels. Jeanne, once an exotic, has one of the finest voices in the music business and has recently made a nationwide tour of the Playboy Clubs and other fine hotels. She's kept just the right touch of sensual movement to complement her fine voice and it looks like she's headed for the top again. I say again, because when Jeanne was an exotic she was rated as one of the country's top ten by *G-String Beat,* a national burlesque column written by Rita Atlanta.

Vegas Visitor

June 23, 1978 Girl watchers are sure to enjoy the dancing talents of the lovely **NICOLE,** one of the featured exotics at the Royal Las Vegas in the "Rare 'N Bare" review staring comic-ventriloquist **LOU DUPONT.**

This lovely lady has a different show for each of her three nightly performances including a gypsy number in a costume of colorful silk scarves gracefully draped about her body and an equally colorful and entertaining Indian number.

Incidentally, those of you in the mood for a bit of comedy will find a new addition to the Maxim's "Olde Tyme Burlesque" show in the Allegro Showroom called "Whistlin' Willy." You won't believe your eyes. Now we know what belly buttons were made for! Credit for this ingenious spoof goes to emcee Teddy King.

And again, back to the girl watchers. Just about any day of the week you'll find a former "Miss Germany" performing at the Cabaret. That's the unpredictable totally madcap **DELILAH JONES** (pictured). This zany lady mixes together music from her homeland and music from Tom Jones and Glen Campbell to come up with totally unique interpretations of the striptease art. Between shows, Delilah keeps herself busy making gorgeous costumes for nearly everyone in the cast.

Vegas Visitor

June 30, 1978 It was a happy occasion when friends and relatives came to the baptizing party for Cynthia Alvita Vespia, the eighth child of **CHARLIE** and **LEONA VESPIA**. There were more than 50 adults and children crowded into Charlie's front room for food and festivities which included the appearance of Whistling Willie also know as **TEDDY KING**, intended for the amusement of the children but everyone enjoyed the performance.

Among the guests were Alvita Lane, Leona's sister and Cynthia's namesake, **CARME**, the child's godfather, Gwen Bernie, the child's godmother, Mr. and Mrs. Irving Benson, **MR. AND MRS. JESS MACK**, Dave Hanson and his wife **SANDY O'HARA**, Cindy Lane, Mrs. And Mrs. Dave Yaquinta, Mr. and Mrs. Teddy King, Eddy Fox, Stacy, Angel Taber, Catherine Taber, Leanora Conley, and many more.

Appearing at the Sneak Joint is the Bobby Durham show featuring **BARBI DOLL**! The talented country western group plays six nights a week with Wednesday night off to give **DARWIN** and his friends room for their weekly magic meeting. Professionals and interested spectators are invited for an evening of fun and entertainment starting at midnight.

Be sure and join us for the final week of "Olde Tyme Burlesque" at the Maxim, starring **BOB MITCHELL** and **CHRISTINE DARLING** and featuring **CHARLIE VESPIA, TRIANA ZZON, P.J. PARKER,** and yours truly!

Vegas Visitor

July 7, 1978 This week finds "Olde Tyme Burlesque" back at the Cabaret Burlesque Palace on Paradise Road. See the whole gang including comic star **BOB MITCHELL,** funny man **CHARLIE VESPIA**, talking woman **CHRISTINE DARLING**, acrobatic **TRIANA ZZON** and yours truly plus additional exotic beauties such as **JAN FONTAINE,** Akiko O'Toole, **ALEXIS**, and more performing nightly.

If you want to impress someone special, why not take him or her to a really unique dining establishment? The one I suggest is Macchiavernas, which not only features some of the most delicious gourmet Italian cuisine I've ever feasted upon, but there are singing waiters, waitresses, and bartenders!

My guest, Triana Zzon and I were really surprised when our waiters, Mark and Dominic (everyone gets two), began singing in front of our table. "I wondered why we got two waiters," was the surprised comment from Triana. While one is singing the other is serving. The musical serenade is to the accompaniment of some fine piano playing by Frank and by Pat.

It is always a treat to see entertainer friends doing something different from what they are generally recognized for. Such is the case of **CARME** (pictured), known as a fine burlesque comic, a talented comic actor at Union Plaza and now the solo opening act for Johnny Harra at the Silverbird.

CARME

Carme has some great comedy material intertwined with a marvelous singing voice. He performs an especially moving version of "My Woman My Woman, My Wife." He also tickles the funny bone with his version of "Green Green Grass of Home."

Carme has performed with many of the biggest "top bananas" in burlesque including Tommy Moe Raft (pictured in a skit called "trying to get arrested"). Carme has also performed with **BILL FANNING** at the Holiday Casino in "Wild World of Burlesque" and again with Bill at the Hacienda in "Love of Sex" which also starred **SANDY O'HARA.** He has also worked with **JIMMY MATTHEWS, CHARLEY VESPIA,** Milt Douglas, Herbie Barris,

Pinky Lee, **TEDDY KING, ARTIE BROOKS** and many more!

Following Carme are the McCoy Sisters, the vocalist trio for Johnny Harra. They opened with "On Broadway" and even added some gospel music.

Then, of course, it is what everyone has been waiting for, the entrance of Johnny as Elvis. Opening in the familiar Elvis style, with the cape and bowing humbly in front of the crowd, Johnny proceeded to sing dozens of the songs Elvis was best known for and which are entirely unnecessary for me to recount. He even gave away several dozen scarves to eagerly awaiting fans.

The resemblance to Elvis is definitely there and many of the audience could be heard whispering that Johnny could pass for Elvis in his last years.

Johnny remarked during his show that he knew there would never be another Elvis, but he hoped he was able to bring back just a few of the great memories. He did!

Did you know that his daughter Lisa Marie won the national look-a-like for Gladys Presley, Elvis' mother? It is eerie watching Johnny, who has been performing his Elvis tribute for the past 18 years, and it is even more unbelievable when you close your eyes and just listen. Thank you Johnny.

Vegas Visitor

July 21, 1978 Lovely **LYNETTE LEAH** (pictured) has joined the day line-up of all-featured exotics at the beautiful Cabaret Club. Lynette has called Hawaii home for the last several years and comes to Las Vegas as part of a national tour and including Canada as well.

Admirers of youth will be delighted in the natural wholesome college girl appeal of Lynette. A very professional exotic, she is also one of the best dressed with wardrobe made by the incomparable **HEDY JO STAR** of Boston.

Bouncy, blonde **FANTASIA** (pictured) is making her exotic debut at the Royal Las Vegas and doing a tremendous job. This former Air Force member (guys keep saying they didn't look like that when they were in the service!) attributes a great deal of her newest show to **LOVEY GOLDMINE,** who for a time, gave lucky girls the benefit of her skills as she choreographed exotic shows and gave girls tips on teasing. Fantasia is certainly a pupil to be proud of and now she's teaching a thing or two about being a very feminine as well as talented dancer.

Also at the Royal is the ever-popular **NICOLE** (pictured). I've seen a vast variety of shows from Nicole, but this was the first time I saw her as a "vamp" and she certainly played the role well.

HEATHER MINSKY looks lovelier than ever and is still being held over at the Royal along with comedy star **LOU DUPONT** who tells me he's perfecting a new dummy (he's a ventriloquist). This dummy will be a robot and operated from the audience by Lou while he is on stage. Should be very unusual. Look for it soon.

Got a chance to catch the show at the newly opened Reef on Sahara near the Jolly Trolley. Only had time to stay for one of the dancers, **MERRILY** (pictured). She does some excellent baton work as well as some agile acrobatic moves. The club itself is a much more informal atmosphere than most Vegas burlesque clubs and a bit too risqué. Music is provided by a jukebox and the dancers double as cocktail waitresses. It was nice to run into Trudy who just got to Vegas and is working as a cocktail waitress. We worked together in Phoenix, Arizona.

Vegas Visitor

July 1978   Still as vivacious and beautiful as ever is the zany and thoroughly entertaining **TRACY SUMMERS**, one of the featured attractions in the day show at the Cabaret. Driving through Las Vegas, you've probably seen Tracy on dozens of billboards and she has been seen in a multitude of magazines and articles about Las Vegas, including a pictorial in a book by Mario Puzo. Just recently someone asked if the girl in Mario's book was me. As a matter of fact, I am honored to say that when I first came to town, some of my friends thought the girl on the billboard was me, but, alas no! We do share the same hairstyle, the same last name, and the same love for having a good time onstage!

Tracy is very creative and versatile. In one show, she's the sultry lady of the night, the next she's a gypsy woman, the next she's the girl from outer space. She genuinely enjoys her work on stage and it certainly shows both in her sunshine smile and in the enthusiastic response she draws from even the quietest audiences.

Finally got a chance to check out the Girl Trap (formerly the Tender Trap). For a Thursday night, they had a fair crowd but could use better dancers.

"Give 'em some more," so say the Platters now packing them in at the Allegro Lounge in the Maxim Hotel. And with their string of hits including "The Great Pretender," "Boogie Man," "I'm Easy," "Silhouettes," and so many more, their enthusiastic crowd didn't want to let them off stage and gave them a rousing standing ovation which was well-deserved by this hard working, great sounding group. After shows, they are available to sign autographs and their albums are also available for sale.

Vegas Visitor

July 28, 1978   As any entertainer can tell you, life in show business for all its rewards is not an easy one. You are subjected daily to disappointments, abuses, uncertainties, unnatural highs and rock bottom lows. Is it no wonder that the entertainer may, in desperation, seek a way to relieve himself or herself of some of that burden by having a drink to "unwind" or a pill to "relax" and another one to get him that additional burst of energy that may make the difference between anonymity and super-stardom?

This story is a special one because it involves a close friend and a courageous woman, **JONI MITCHELL**. In past columns you've seen her featured at the Jolly Trolley and she worked with me at the Royal Las Vegas. She also featured at Circus Circus. She was, in fact, one of Las Vegas' leading most talented exotics. Was? Yes, that's right. Joni is now a counselor for Community Referral Services, also known as Court Referral Service (CRS).

CRS is a non-profit organization dedicated to helping people help themselves, with prime emphasis on the abuse of alcohol and other drugs. Joni came to their attention and influence through the usual manner – a DWI; traffic court.

"I had been drinking and taking just about anything I could find," admits Joni, "since I was about 22. I felt worthless and I didn't think anyone could or would want to help me.

The people at CRS are just great. They taught me to like myself, to find my own way. For the first time in my life, someone understood me. They were willing to listen. And so importantly, they didn't put me down at anytime. Everything they said and did was so positive. I couldn't help but feel great. I found I didn't need to get high anymore, I felt too good!"

After Joni demonstrated her success with the program at CRS, which has only been in existence five years, Paul Casey, her personal counselor, and Ray Harris, the executive director, suggested that Joni might get involved herself. She could help others through her own experiences.

"In this program, it is not the amount of formal education you have," explains Joni, "our best counselors have been people just like me. People who can relate because they've been there. At CRS, they saw my potential and they loved me when I didn't. All the positive feelings and knowledge I got from CRS is what I want to share with others and to let them know someone really does care."

Some of the people whom Joni would like to express her gratitude to include: Ray Harris, Paul Casey, Yvonne Baker, Joan Higginson, Russ Schoenbeck, Paul Faulkner, Gina Carroll, Judy Elmore, Lydia, Reese, Garland Grizzel and Bud Hodges. Congratulations to Joni in your success with CRS.

Vegas Visitor

August 4, 1978 "Minsky's Burlesque Follies" starring Irving Benson and **CASSANDRA LEE** is in its second week at the Maxim Hotel.

The show also features lovely redhead **CIMMARON** who just closed at the Royal Las Vegas. Cimmaron does a cute Red Riding Hood number climaxed with some graceful prop acrobatics.

There is a full chorus line choreographed by Betty Francisco and costumed by Eastwood. I am not a really qualified critic when it comes to chorus line dancing but I just didn't find any pizzazz in their numbers with the exception of a beautifully executed adagio number with Michael, lead dancer, and two male dancers, Kurt and Ron.

There is some old time comedy in the show with Irving Benson performing the comedy honors aided by straight man, Jerry Lucas, also the shows

producer. While I found Irving to be a very funny man, I thought he could have used more help from his straight man who was just a little bit too straight. He almost read his lines.

Cassandra is featured throughout the show in routines with the chorus line but when it comes to her own spot, she is definitely a knock out! As many times as I've seen her, this is by far her best and most elegant performance!

One of the funniest and most entertaining plays to hit Vegas has to be "Pajama Tops" now at the Union Plaza. It stars buxom June Wilkinson but the show is "stolen" by William Browder in his performance as Leonard JoliJoli. Incidentally, William is the director of this hilarious farce as well. Be sure and see it!

The Improvisation, the world-famous New York nitery that launched the careers of many stars, will be opening its third club in Las Vegas in mid-August in the Commercial Center. Neil Philips, one of the owners, is currently auditioning comedians, singers, comedy groups, and novelty acts for the premier showcase.

Judy Wolfe has been named Director of Publicity and Advertising for the Ambassador Inn. Wolfe has been doing lots of freelance publicity for a variety of entertainers and will begin her new position by promoting the grand opening activities of the Ambassador Inn's new casino, coffee shop, and lounge scheduled for September 8.

Vegas Visitor

August 25, 1978   There's new things happening at the Landmark and much of it is credited to show room star and host, **GEORGE KIRBY** (pictured). In a concept generally familiar only to the smaller and more intimate night-clubs, George acts as host throughout the show which features the singing talents of LaVonne Elliott, the unbelievable gymnastics of the 3rd Generation Steps, and singing star Eddie Kendricks with his own back-up group, in addition to the 15-piece Hoyt Henry Orchestra.

Currently appearing at the Ambassador is Trisha Lynn with an astounding 300-song repertoire of tunes from the 1940s to present day rock in addition to the songs she sings in French.

I took a short holiday to Disneyland and to the Hollywood area and finally had a chance to catch the exotic show at the famous Body Shop in Hollywood. I guess you get spoiled in Vegas but after hearing about the famous Sunset Strip all my life, I was really disappointed. Vegas entertainers will be happy to know the Sunset Strip is lined with billboards advertising Las Vegas!

Known primarily for his comic ability, George surprised much of his audience with some fantastic song styles, most notably, Barry Manilow's "I Write the songs." George was the first artist to perform the song on television when he taped a Mike Douglas special.

Throughout the show, George's easygoing manner led the way through some really impressive talents. LaVonne Elliott visibly moved the audience with "I Wish You Love." 3rd Generation Steps tap-danced, did walkovers, flips, splits, and other impossible to describe movements one right after the other and were joined onstage by their father!

Eddie Kendricks, along with Maude Mobley and Janet Wright, did several of the tunes the Temptations were so well known for, and just as I remarked on the similarity of voices to my companion, Eddie told the audience he used to sing with another group – The Temptations! Eddie has one of those purely melodious voices like bells tinkling and he treats the audience to his wide variety of arrangements including: "Just My Imagination," "Keep On Truckin'," and the most beautiful of all, "Best of Strangers."

And there's an unexpected guest too, George's son Bob McDonald with some good impressions of Muhammad Ali, Sidney Portier and Bill Cosby, leading directly to George's own impersonations of Boris Karloff, Jimmy Cagney, and Pearl Baily. George also impersonates the sax and the bass!

George plans much more in the future at the Landmark too. "I'm going to keep our shows at 10 PM and 2:30AM to give some of the folks who work the Strip a chance to see a full production show. On Monday nights our show is dark and I plan to feature a different jazz group every week, including Buddy Rich, Lionel Hampton, Woody Herman, and Count Basie.

"I intend to keep the nucleus of my show intact and bring in additional new talent often. This week we're bringing in the "Let It Be Lowenbrau" voice of Arthur Prycock and comedian Irwin C. Watson."

Following that will be a show called "Beatlefever." It's a live simulation capturing the original sights and sounds of the great Beatles, something a little different from all the Elvis imitators. I'm also negotiating for talents like Ray Charles and with Paul Atkins to televise that show from the Landmark. I even plan to bring in some of the contestants from the Gong Show."

George expresses a strong interest in bringing new talent to Vegas. "Seems like every time I'm flying, someone asks me who is playing in Las Vegas and after I recite the names, they say, "Are they still there?" Seems like everyone's afraid to try somebody new and there's a lot of talent out there waiting for a chance to be heard."

Note: It took awhile to get this interview because George Kirby was arrested in a drug bust behind Jerry's Nugget the day before my scheduled interview. He made bail and my interview was rescheduled. According to Wikipedia, George served 42 months of a ten-year sentence. After prison, he made a few television appearances and continued to perform stand-up, never attaining his pre-drug bust popularity. In later years he was diagnosed with Parkinson's disease and died in 1995.

Vegas Visitor

September 1, 1978   There's more comedy than ever at the Cabaret Burlesque Palace featuring **BOB MITCHELL, CHARLIE VESPIA, TEDDY KING,** and **BRANDY DURAN** (Brandy is pictured), in the classic *transformer* scene.

Additionally, *ANGELIQUE PET-TYJOHN* is doing the honors with Bob and Charlie in the *movie scene* and the *crazy house*. All of the skits feature the rest of the all-star exotic cast in walk-ons.

GINA BON BON is back from another road tour that took her to Grand Rapids, Chattanooga, Nashville, Dallas, and many more. After a week or two loafing around home, Gina will be opening in Las Vegas.

BRANDI DURAN

Labeled by TV Guide as "one of the most talented ventriloquists to graduate from the teacher that schooled Edgar Bergan," Stu Scott and his animals, George the Cocky Crow and Barney the Booze Frog, will be opening in "Razzle Dazzle," September 1 at the Flamingo Hilton.

Bob Mitchell and his lovely wife Joni used to live in Dallas before coming to Las Vegas and Bob says they were always looking for something to do, so they both earned certificates in dog trimming and they also attended beauty college. "I have over 500 hours," says Bob. "They used to request me for shampoos. That was a big first for the college. Normally everyone has a request for a certain student to do their hair but with me it was shampoos."

Want to know where to find some good go-go dancers? Try the Gilded

Cage in North Las Vegas. It's right across the street from Jerry's Nugget on Las Vegas Blvd.

When I saw "Fantasy On Ice" at the Hacienda, I thought one of the girls looked familiar but her name wasn't on the table cards. I've since verified that it was **JUDY MICHAELS**, the talented redhead who has been featured in dozens of hotels on the strip and most recently was the emcee at the Joker Club and the Cabaret. Judy is a talented choreographer, dancer, and ice skater.

Vegas Visitor

September 15, 1978   JUDY MICHAELS has just opened at the Jolly Trolley after closing as one of the skating stars at the Hacienda. The lovely red head is one of Vegas' most popular and talented dancers and has been featured in many of the major hotels as well as many television shows and movies, most notably as a dancer in "Bye Bye Birdie."

I hear that the new show at the Fremont, "Space Circus," is really good. That comes from Dick McNeely, owner of the paper that is distributed in all the taxicabs.

Got a chance to check out Billy Bo's and found it to be a delightful place, cozy with lush décor, live and disco music, a dance floor to be envied by clubs four times its size and friendly go-go girls who double as cocktail waitresses. It's really worth a stop.

Everyone keeps asking about my new book and I think I've probably told a dozen other columnists but neglected to write about it myself! Anyway, the book is called *How To Be A Professional Stripper* written by me and illustrated by **TRIANA ZZON.**

The book is a good handbook for would-be-strippers in that I've given lists of top-notch agents, costume makers, publicity photographers, and other information on how to get started. From anyone's point of view, it is interesting reading to get some of the picture of just what goes into a show, what kind of conditions many exotics work under, what they can achieve in salary, and the various laws regarding burlesque state to state and even city to city. For instance, did you know that in Orlando, Florida you may go completely nude but in Tampa you must wear G-strings and pasties; or that in E. Dubuque, Illinois all the clubs must have the front window uncovered so the interior of the club is visible from the street? Passerby's can sort of window shop!

The book is available at the Cabaret and Palomino box offices for $2.50 or through the mail (C/O Vegas Visitor) for $2.98, which includes postage and handling and even an autograph if you wish.

Attended the opening of the Improvisation with friends **MR. AND MRS. JESS MACK,** Mr. and Mrs. Sy Newman, Dick McNeely, Ted Whetstone, **GYPSY LOUISE**, Judy Wolfe and **SUSI MIDNIGHT**. Peer Marini provided the music. Comics and singers were booked in locally and from the Improvisations in Los Angeles, and New

York City. I most enjoyed singer Ruth Randolph who did a sexy rendition of "Goody Goody" and an upcoming young comic named Ed Bluestone who has already had appearances on Laugh In, The Tonight Show, and Merv Griffin. He's also appeared at the LA Improvisation.

Vegas Visitor

September 22, 1978 **MISS NUDE UNIVERSE – KITTEN NATIVIDAD** (pictured) is now appearing In a special two-week engagement at the newly remodeled Joker Club in the popular "Olde Tyme Burlesque" review which stars **BOB MITCHELL** and **CHARLIE VESPIA.**

Kitten is one of the top stars in Russ Meyers' sexy films and with her 40-20-34 dimensions, it's easy to understand why. She was seen recently in "Up" at the El Portal Theatre here and is the star in "Beneath the Valley of the Ultra Vixen" which will be released soon. In this Russ Meyers production, Kitten plays duo roles as a hillbilly and as a Spanish lass. She also helped write the script, which is based on her own hilarious sexcapades!

There are lots of new faces in the "Olde Tyme Burlesque" show including **ANGELIQUE PETTIJOHN,** best known for her many acting roles including co-starring on Star Trek, **BRANDY DURAN,** a Minsky's star, and **TERI STARR,** "The Heavenly Body." Yours truly will also be there to add a touch of magic and give a hand in the hilarious old time burlesque skits that have made our show such a popular one. Emcee is **TEDDY KING.**

"**SPACE CIRCUS**" is the new show in the lounge at the Fremont Hotel and due to the enthusiastic response, it is slated for an indefinite engagement.

Conceived and directed by Joey Skilbred and produced by Ronnie Kirtz and Tony Rome, the one hour show is filled with fantastic costumes from outer space, lots of gorgeous girls, comedy and a sexy young man named Steve Scott, the only "strong man strip" in burlesque!

Steve plays the good guy in the production numbers, a space counterpart to the knight in shining armor of old. In his strip sequence, Steve, who is a disarmingly good looking blonde, is undressed by the female members of the cast and then proceeds to show us why he, as "The Flash," is known for his unsurpassed strength. He starts by taking a solid steel bar that he passes through the audience to verify its authenticity and then he bends it completely in two. He then passes a five-gallon hot water bottle to the audience and upon its return he proceeds to blow it up AND completely apart!

Laughs in the show are furnished by Ricci Carr who does a marvelous belly dance complete with belly roll and combat boots! Later in the show, he also makes a grand appearance as a butterfly (moth)!

Dancers in the show include Tanya Stevens, Linda London, April Maitland, and Jocelyn Summers.

"Space Circus" is one of the most original shows I've seen in Vegas and the cast deserves congratulations on a thoroughly entertaining show.

Vegas Visitor

September 27, 1978 Creating chaos wherever she appears, **ANN MARIE** (pictured), 67-25-36, is America's number one exotic attraction and opens Jan, 31 in the Allegro Lounge of the Maxim Hotel in "Olde Tyme Burlesque" also starring comic **BOB MITCHELL** and featuring **CHARLIE VESPIA. CHRISTINE DARLING** will be the talking lady for the classic burlesque skits and the show will be rounded out with the performances of exotics **TRIANA ZZON** and yours truly.

The multi-talented Ann Marie will be giving audiences a lot for their money. Besides the obvious, she is a creative dancer, singer, and comedienne as well as an actress having been featured in several Russ Meyers films.

Everyone will enjoy the comical antics of Bob Mitchell and Charlie Vespia, with the assistance of Christine Darling, as they cavort their way through the wildest comedy scenes in burlesque. Additionally, there is Charlie with his unexpectedly fine talents as an operatic singer and Bob who plays two and three horns simultaneously.

The lithe and lovely brunette **TRI-ANNA ZZON** (pictured) is a very graceful and amazing acrobatic dancer. She got her start in show business via backstage duties at the Third Eye Theatre, a legitimate playhouse in Denver, Colorado where she served in various roles as wardrobe mistress, costume designer, and stage manager, giving her an in-depth study of behind the lights action.

A hunger for some of the limelight took Triana to San Francisco where she first got a job at a recording studio as secretary. "Mostly, they had me listen to recordings and give my opinion. I was more a critic than a secretary."

From there, Triana gave North Beach a try, performing as a nude dancer in clubs such as Coke's, the Condor, El Cid's and the Off Broadway.

"I worked with people who helped and inspired me as I got my own act together. I filled in for Carol Doda at the Condor. I got to see Tempest Storm when she appeared in San Francisco."

Triana credits Hully Feticio, manager of the Off Broadway and a former dancer who had worked with Sammy Davis Jr., as giving her the most help.

"He was fantastic, an incredible dancer, and he worked my tail off. I learned a lot."

Triana's next move was to Los Angeles to be with some of her family. While there, she landed the feature spot at the Arches in the valley where she was held over a year and a half until her move to Las Vegas in October.

"I'd known **SNOWY SINCLAIR** (appears at the Cabaret) for a long time so I knew there were places to work in Vegas and I wanted to give it a try."

Vegas Visitor

September 29, 1978   The word is out and that word is "smashing, " which describes the most successful show to hit the Joker Club, "Olde Tyme Burlesque," starring **BOB MITCHELL, CHARLIE VESPIA** and featuring the extraordinary talents of "Miss Nude Universe," the vivacious **KITTEN.**

The one hour 45 minute show is packed with five burlesque classic scenes, the musical talents of Bob Mitchell, a stand-up routine with Bob Mitchell and **TEDDY KING**, even a bath on stage with Kitten. During the very brief intermission, lovely Katina, the cocktail waitress, surprises her customers with a scintillating performance. Catch all the excitement three times nightly!

Heard a great story the other day about **SUSI MIDNIGHT**, one of the exotic stars at the Palomino. Seems several years ago, Susi, who could win a

An audition with **PAUL PERRY** landed her a spot for his review at the Cabaret and a chance to learn some of the burlesque skits being presented nightly.

We will all be looking forward to seeing you at our opening at the Maxim on January 31. Show times will be 8:30, midnight, and 2:30. Please come!

demolition derby hands down, bought a new car. She was worried that she might dent her new car.

One night she left work only to return two hours later and she left again with Jack Perry. Everyone was curious. Seems that Susi got home and there was only one parking place, parallel between two cars, which was only big enough to park a tank in but Susi didn't want to risk a try so she drove around the block for an hour and a half hoping someone would vacate a space in the parking lot. When no one did, she went back to the club and got Jack so that he could come and park her car for her!

Get well wishes go to Joni Mitchell, recuperating at home after a weeks stay in the hospital. She's fine and getting better.

Congratulations to **DOROTHY AND JESS MACK** who are celebrating their tenth wedding anniversary!

Vegas Visitor

October 6, 1978   Miss Nude Hawaii, **LA LANEAH LEE** (pictured), is now appearing at the Cabaret Burlesque Palace, bringing with her a variety of entertaining routines and some beautiful wardrobe.

The talented miss was born in Korea but was raised in Hawaii. She studied art and interior decorating which she plans to take up again when she quits dancing some time in the far future!

137

LA LANEAH LEE

Currently purchasing a home in Las Vegas where she plans to spend her winters, La Laneah also has a home in Milwaukee where she will spend her summers. She finds the cold weather in Wisconsin too hard on her body.

Her shows include the current rage for the 50s with music from Grease and some Elvis selections, a little girl show using Lily Tomlin's famous Edith Ann characterization, and of course, a Hawaiian show, plus many more.

If you're interested in being a masseuse you should catch Joni Walkers show at the Palomino. She should be doing commercials for Jergens!

Also at the Palomino is the sentimental lady **LISA LAMONTE** (pictured).

This beautiful brunette also has a wide variety of shows to please you and you can catch her any afternoon from 2PM.

The night show at the Palomino is happy to have back their favorite blonde, **BARBI DOLL,** who has been on vacation in Cleveland, Ohio.

SUZETTE SUMMERS can be found titillating the lucky patrons of the Jolly Trolley along with the lovely redhead **JUDY MICHAELS** and pretty Tiffany Holiday.

LISA LAMONTE

SHE BABETTE entertains at the Reef, one of the newest burlesque clubs. And you will find lovely **DEIRDRE RHODES** at the Crazy Horse Saloon along with dozens of other go-go dancers and exotics.

Vegas Visitor

October 13, 1978 Formerly a schoolteacher and stage actress in her native Puerto Rico, black-haired beauty **MARGARITA RIVERA** (pictured), is now giving a Latin flavor to the exotic line-up at the Palomino Club nightly.

Margarita is, of course, a college graduate. Before she came to this country she taught Spanish and drama in the daytime while she performed in stage productions of several plays in the evenings.

She came to America 2 ½ years ago, intending to pursue a doctorate in literature at the University of La Jolla in San Diego. Arriving a couple of months early, she found there was no employment for someone with her qualifications. She needed to be re-certified to teach here and this was further complicated by her inability to speak English.

Eventually she got a job as a go-go dancer in Los Angeles. Friends she'd made in San Diego persuaded her to return and perform in nightclubs there, which she eventually did, going on to feature at Les Girls, The Alley Cat, The Star and Garter, and several other top clubs. During this time she also met and married her husband who is a craps dealer at the Jolly Trolley.

Curiosity brought her and her new husband to Las Vegas almost a year ago. When asked if she planned to make Vegas her permanent home, Margarita replied, "I haven't really put my roots down but as long as Vegas keeps being good to me as it has, I'll stay."

I asked Margarita if she still had trouble with English and in a delightful accent she answered, "I don't understand too well, when people start talking real fast and sometimes I don't understand the different meanings for the same things."

Margarita said that Puerto Rico was very Americanized so she didn't have too hard a time when it came to American food but she finds it difficult to find good Mexican restaurants here! (Note) I guess I'm spoiled by El Jardins but on a recent trip to Mexico, I found I definitely prefer Americanized Mexican food!

Margarita makes her own elaborate wardrobe with Latin styling and selects her music from the Fania label where she finds a large variety of Latin artists to compliment her scintillating shows.

On stage, she says she forgets that she's supposed to be a sex symbol. "I've always been very shy, so each show is a real challenge to me. I forget about feeling sexy and concentrate on entertaining. I guess that's partly due to my theatrical training."

In her spare time, Margarita enjoys writing and has written several plays. She has had several of her articles published in Puerto Rico. Someday she'd like to continue a career in literature.

One of her favorite pastimes is just going to the desert. "I get such a feeling of peace," she explains.

Put a little spice in your life and plan to see Margarita at the Palomino along with an all-star exotic line-up and the world famous amateur nude dance contest.

Vegas Visitor

October 20, 1978 "Olde Tyme Burlesque" is back at the Maxim Hotel. This exceptionally entertaining show first ran at the Maxim for almost six months and from there went to the Cabaret and the Joker Club. And now, with even more talented performers and more comedy than ever, "Olde Tyme Burlesque" is back!

The featured exotic is the lovely **ANGELIQUE PETTIJOHN**. She will re-create "Shanna" (pictured), the character she brought to life in her starring role on Star Trek. She helped Captain Kirk escape after his imprisonment by her masters.

Angelique has enlisted the aid of Trekkie fans, who have furnished her

with stills of the episode, so that she might capture the exact likeness of the green-haired lovely down to the costume she wore for the episode and she has chosen some props and music to set it all off.

Angelique, who has been compared to beauties like Sharon Tate and Raquel Welch, has had many featured film roles including "Hell's Bells," "President's Analyst," "Guide for the Married Man," "Clambake," "Gypsy Moth," "Tell Me That You Love Me, Junie Moon," "Rough Night in Jericho," and "The Love God." Angelique has dozens of television credits including many more roles on "Star Trek." She's been in "Love American Style," "Bracken's World," "Good Morning World," "Pruitts of South Hampton," "Mr. Terrific," "Green Hornet," "Batman," "Girl From Uncle," and "Get Smart."

Additionally, Angelique has been featured in most of the top burlesque shows in Las Vegas including Barry Ashton's "Wonderful World of Burlesque" at the Aladdin, Minsky's at the Silver Slipper and Thunderbird as well as the Flamingo.

"Olde Tyme Burlesque," as the name implies, contains the classics of burlesque comedy skits. In addition to the popular "movie" and "crazy house" scenes, performed in the last outing at the Maxim, several new skits have been added including "trying to get arrested," and the "transformer" scene. **BRANDY DURAN** is the featured talking woman to comedy stars **BOB MITCHELL** and

CHARLIE VESPIA. Straight man, emcee **TEDDY KING,** will also be performing his unforgettable "Whistling Willie."

Also performing will be yours truly featuring my beautiful white doves in some magic illusions as well as other effects and having the honor of performing in the skits as well.

Although it may rightfully be argued that since I appear in this production, my opinions are prejudiced, I do want to say that this is the most fun show I've ever worked in and I think we can all agree that if the cast is having a good time so will you.

Vegas Visitor

October 27, 1978 The "Love Potion Girl" **MISS GINA BON BON** (pictured), is back in Las Vegas and performing at the Joker Club. This

Cuban beauty is one of the countries most popular and best-known exotics and puts on a great show. Her wardrobe alone is worth the visit.

Also appearing at the Joker Club are **TERI STARR, K.C. LAYNE, FANTASIA** and Las Vegas' newest exotic Katina. Katina was a cocktail waitress at the club and would occasionally dance between shows. She did such a fine job, owner **PAUL PERRY** took notice of her and invited her to turn professional.

DI ALBA (pictured) is back at the Cabaret. One of these days some movie producer is going to catch a glimpse of her flawlessly beautiful face and add another sensational lady to the ranks of Brigette Bardot and Sophia Loren.

"Razzle Dazzle" at the Flamingo Hilton certainly lives up to its name. Amid all the feathers and rhinestones on the skating beauties you will also find an unforgettable evening of entertainment.

The outstanding spot in the show for me was Dominique. Billed as "The Pickpocket Extraordinaire" and starring in the show, Dominique chose several audience participants and deftly picked off their watches, wallets, combs, belts and even one guy's shirt and t-shirt. Along with an illusion using a female audience participant and some classical guitar, Dominique presents a completely entertaining and exciting performance.

Catch drummer Mike Leonetti at the Fremont's Carnival Room. The show is a tribute to the 1940s era including the songs of Al Jolson and Louis Prima. The big band era is a natural for Mike in that his grandfather played with Gene Krupa.

There are three shows nightly except Thursday. While you're there stay awhile and catch the mini-review "Space Circus."

Vegas Visitor

November 3, 1978 Beautiful "Miss Nude Universe," also known as **KITTEN** (pictured), has returned to the Joker Club after a short vacation in Los Angeles. Watch for the release of Russ Meyer's production "Beneath the Valley of the Dolls" in which Kitten has the starring role.

Kitten helped write the script and plays the duo roles of a hillbilly with a southern drawl and a Spanish lass with a Spanish accent.

KITTEN NATIVIDAD

"It's really a challenge to my abilities as an actress," says Kitten. "It helps that a lot of the script is based on my own hilarious sexual escapades," explains the uninhibited exotic star.

Kitten plans on making Las Vegas her second home and recently purchased a large home with a swimming pool. Neighbors are in for a real treat as the home is fenced with cyclone fencing around the backyard where the pool is located and Kitten just loves sun bathing!

LOU DUPONT continues to keep folks in stiches as the star of "Rare 'n Bare" at the Royal Las Vegas. I understand that in addition to being a talented comic-ventriloquist, Lou is quite a businessman and owns several shops and apartment buildings around Las Vegas.

DOROTHY and **JESS MACK** are the people to see in Las Vegas for the top names in burlesque as well as variety acts, actresses, and actors. They are currently helping to cast several television and movie productions filming in Las Vegas.

The cast of "Old Tyme Burlesque" was honored to have Telly Savalas as a guest during one of their recent performances. A mark of a successful show is the number of other entertainers who come to see it and "Olde Tyme Burlesque" has numbered in its audience such notables as June Allyson, Jack Kelly, Tony Curtis, Tomsoni and many many more. We'd love to have you!

Vegas Visitor

November 1978 One of the dancing stars of the "Rare'N Bare" show at the Royal Las Vegas is lovely **ROBIN-O** (pictured) who got her start singing and dancing in her father's supper club in Ogden, Utah where she also had to wash dishes and wait on the customers.

That start, however, was the inspiration that brought her to Las Vegas and her first job in the Rocky Sennes production of the "Tom Jones Review" at the Holiday Casino. A touch of the big time and Robin was hooked.

After the Holiday came a stint as a chorus line dancer for two years with the famous "Minskys Review" during which she toured to Miami Beach, Washington D.C., Boston and New York City.

Theatrical agent George Soares sent Robin to Reno as an exotic dancer for the Holiday Casino. Robin then joined Marc Anthony, former singing star of "Casino De Paris," and with him, sang and danced for several months. Then she was off to exotic places like Dublin, Ireland, and London, England for an engagement with the Fiesta Clubs.

Upon her return to Las Vegas, Robin decided that performing solo was what she really wanted to do. "I love to create my own fantasies for the audience to enjoy," explains Robin, who closes the show at the Royal Las Vegas.

Robin joined **CASSANDRA LEE** and **SUZETTE SUMMERS** to produce "Fantasy Follies" which had a lengthy and successful run at the Jolly Trolley and gave her the show name Robin-O. Robin is a naturally soft and pretty redhead who never stops moving and who makes each movement count. She combines the right touch of tease and dancing talent for an altogether alluring routine.

In her spare time, Robin also sews and designs the costumes she wears, enjoys gourmet cooking, dance classes, and jogging. She also plays the piano and sings, enjoying mostly country western with a little Bach and Beethoven on the side.

Another exciting exotic in the show is Heather Minsky, the "Lola of Burlesque." There is also former Fremont Hotel star, Linda London – "The Girl With The Hair." In fact she gives the infamous Farrah Fawcett more than a run for the money. And still with

the show is the vivacious **NICOLE** with a new routine called "Money, Money," performing it so well that some of the counterfeit bills she hands out are replaced by the customers with real money!

The star of this beauty packed show is ventriloquist **LOU DUPONT**, keeping the audience in tears of laughter as he deftly manipulates three of the most unusual dummies I've ever seen. You'll understand the comment more when you see one of the dummies "Chewchie."

Vegas Visitor

November 1978 "The Sexiest Gal in Town" **HOLLY CARROLL** (pictured), super talented singer and dancer, will open in Frankie Carr's production of "Le Whoopee" at Joe Julian's November 15.

Holly, a green-eyed strawberry blonde, just finished her second engagement at the Bingo Palace where she gave audiences a treat nightly with her sultry delivery of such classics as "Ain't Misbehavin" and "Sexiest Girl In Town." She also added some high kicking, high stepping dancing to her delivery of "New York, New York."

Holly has been considering several recording offers as well as offers for songs she's written, one of the best being "What Good is Love." As far as her dancing career goes, that's far from over. In "Le Whoopee," in addition to her spot as featured vocalist, Holly will also be featured exotic dancer. "I love dancing," admits Holly. "I don't think I could ever give it up entirely and I think it helps sell my songs."

One of the best lounge bargains in town as well as one of the most entertaining has to be the lounge at the Silverbird featuring the Pete Wilcox show. Pete performs a variety of songs and adds some incredible impressions including Nixon and the Tricky Dick Singers. He also does a great Elvis impersonation complete with the rhinestone jeweled pantsuits Elvis was so identified with and the inevitable scarf hanging loosely from his neck. It's a great hour of entertainment with no cover or minimum.

Vegas Visitor

December 7, 1978 Once known as the "Barrymore's of Burlesque", the Graham Family is alive and well and lending at least some of their charms to Las Vegas. I am referring specifically to **P.J. PARKER** at the Cabaret and her sister, **AMBER LYNN** (pictured) at the Maxim Hotel.

MURRAY LANGSTON, 'The Unknown Comic,' who stars frequently at the Sahara's Casbar Theater, is writing his second movie script entitled "the Unknown Comic Movie" in which he will play a cop during the day that is a comic at night.

See some of the prettiest and most talented dancers in town at the Golden Eagle (formerly Jolly Trolley) every day from noon to six in the morning. And while you're at it, stop in and say hi to me. I will be performing at 8PM, 10:30PM and 1AM nightly.

The Graham Family includes their mother Ava Leigh, father Gene Graham and brother Jack Graham. For years, the Graham's were billed around the country as "The Barrymore's of Burlesque." They starred in all the top nightspots in the east. Leon Miller, one of burlesque's best known producers, staged and directed a production called "South Terrific (South Pacific)" around the Graham family and starring Amber whose stage name at the time was Amber Delight.

I asked Amber if it was a bit difficult working for her parents. "Well, yes and no," was her reply. "We have always been a close family so we got along well. But my parents did expect us to set an example for the rest of the cast."

Amber and P.J. joined the burlesque circuit with their parents during the last couple of years of summer vacation from the Catholic boarding school they attended.

"I don't know what they would have thought at school about us working in a burlesque show," says Amber. "All year long we were taught a very careful and precise set of rules and then all summer worked burlesque. But it was fun."

In 1969, the Grahams came to Las Vegas to attend a convention of the outdoor show people. While here, the Grahams went to work for **PAUL PERRY** at his newly opened Palomino Club where they played for three weeks. By now they knew they wanted to make Las Vegas their permanent home but they had to go back east to fulfill prior contracts.

Upon returning, Amber and P.J. went back to work for Paul with Ava Leigh making frequent appearances.

Eventually, P.J. married Vegas Vampire Jim Parker and shortly thereafter a knee injury retired her from the stage until about a year ago.

In 1972, Amber married and quit dancing a year later while she awaited her first son. After her son was born, Amber became a dealer at the Royal Inn where her brother Jack worked as the head of the slot department. She went from there to deal at the Joker Club. She retired from dealing a couple of years later to await the arrival of twins!

"Then Frank and I separated and with three kids, I had to go back to work. Since Paul had replaced me long ago at the Joker and there was a vacancy in the light department, here I am," declares Amber.

Amber confessed that she prefers lighting the show to dealing anyway. "It is more interesting and I get a chance to be creative."

She also performs in some of the burlesque scenes in "Olde Tyme Burlesque." "That's what I really enjoy the most, always did."

Does Amber want to return to the stage as a dancer? She is undecided at the moment. "I enjoy what I'm doing now, but you can never tell, " Amber is leaving just a bit of hope for all those burlesque fans!

Vegas Visitor

December 15, 1978 **SHE BABETTE** (pictured) is among the line-up of lovely exotics currently being featured at the all-new Joker Club in North Las Vegas across from the Palomino.

You can also see the delightful **TERI STARR**, the "love-potion candy girl, **GINA BON BON, FANTASIA,** Anneka, and all the way from Germany, the lovely Marion. The excitement begins nightly at 8PM except Sunday.

Coming to town with holiday spirit and appearing at the Palomino December 18-24, is Candy Samples. She is Southern California's leading exotic. Candy has a busy schedule of movie appearances in films such as "Flesh Gordon," "Captain Hook," and "Beneath the Valley of the Ultra Vixen," by **RUSS MEYERS**. She also has plans for a tour of the Orient. Candy says she likes gambling in Vegas and you will like the sweetness of Candy Samples.

An especially talented duo, Streetcar is performing in the lounge at the Maxim Hotel. Stop in and hear such favorites as "Blue Bayou," "Boring Rendezvous," and selections from "Saturday Night Fever." They play rock, pop and country.

While you are at the Maxim you can stop in and say hi to me and the rest of the cast of "Olde Tyme Burlesque" in the Allegro Showroom. We will be sharing the bill starting December 12 with the marvelous Platters. That should provide you with a full evenings entertainment!

SHE BABETTE

Frederick Apcar's award winning "Bare Touch of Vegas' at the Marina has added some great novelty to their already exciting review. I am speaking of Ricco, the electrifying magician and the hilariously zany Bizzards, three comics who make music in the most unusual ways!

Recently enjoyed the always-entertaining Pin-Ups at the Sahara Casbar. Question: Who scalped Peter Anthony?

American Singing Telegrams is having a grand opening December 17. They are located in the Commercial Center Shopping Center above Lam's Chinese Kitchen. It's a great idea to add an unusual touch to any occasion.

Vegas Visitor

December 1978 "Direct from Las Vegas, Nevada, an X-rated comedienne and exotic dancer rolled into 450 pounds of loveable flesh, the dynamic **BIG FANNIE ANNIE** (pictured)." And so goes the introduction to the stage of the Golden Banana in Boston of this week's newest attraction.

And does Annie do what the rest of the girls do? You bet! And more! And totally nude as well!

First Annie struts her stuff across the stage, surprisingly agile for her weight and size and six foot frame. To a variety of music including David Rose's "Stripper", Annie proceeds to bump and grind and remove her clothing, adding some boob flexing just for fun. Then she grabs the microphone and gives her nearly hysterical audience hell!

Annie started her entertainment career several years ago as a go-go dancer in Miami when she was laid off her job as a secretary for United Airlines during a strike. The comedy business is relatively new, just about nine months new in fact. And it seems to supply the necessary spark to make Annie a sure hit. Although Annie does not yet have a lot of material, she is reasonably good at ad-libbing and comebacks and her size certainly helps keep the audience's attention.

In entertainment, it always helps to have a gimmick to attract attention and talk and Fannie certainly has a gimmick she doesn't have to worry much about being duplicated. She's attracted enough attention to get several television appearances and also won a beauty title – Miss World Belly Flop 1979 – which you'll see on NBC in January.

Aspirations? Fannie loves television and would also like a chance in movies. Very confident, Annie says, "You know size doesn't count. A person can be anything they want. Just don't give up – the bigger the better." With that attitude how can she fail?

Vegas Visitor

December 22, 1978 **SANDY O'HARA** (pictured) has returned to Las Vegas after an extensive tour including most of the Midwest and Canada. She brings the elegance and charm of the "Improper Bostonian" to the Cabaret Burlesque Palace. Fans will remember the lovely redhead from her recent appearances at the Holiday Casino and the Silver Slipper.

SANDY O'HARA

Christmas time seems to bring out the giving spirit in everyone, especially when it comes to needy children. If you'd like to help, I have a suggestion. St. Jude's for Children in Boulder City, which is primarily an orphanage, is in need of toys, clothing of all sizes, and foodstuffs, or money donations. Collecting for them is **BARBI DOLL** whom you may contact at the Palomino Club or you may contact me at the Maxim Hotel or send donations to Vegas Visitor.

One of the cutest additions to the Cabaret stage is Diane Fox. This little blonde has only been in burlesque a short time but she has the benefit of older sister **ANGELIQUE PETTI-JOHN'S** (star of "Olde Time Burlesque") help and encouragement and her own marvelously inventive imagination. One of her shows in particular is a real crowd pleaser. She does a complete act of "Little Red Riding Hood" with sound effects, forest scenery, a basket of goodies, and a big bad wolf! You won't see this at Disneyland!

Stu Scott, ventriloquist star at the Flamingo Hilton's "Razzle Dazzle," is going to be included in a new book written by Stanley Burns of New York City with Mark Wade, editor of "The Oracle." It's going to be all about the art of ventriloquism.

Look for the return of the multi-talented **FRED TRAVALENA** (the silver bullet) December 22nd when he co-headlines with Shirley MacLaine at the Riviera. Fred will ring in the holidays with impressions of such greats as Frank Sinatra, Rose Kennedy, and Jimmy Carter as well as dozens of others. His impressions, coupled with magnificent musical arrangements and hilarious stories, should provide you with a thoroughly entertaining evening.

Vegas Visitor

1978 Soft and sexy **STAR ANN** (pictured), now dancing at the Golden Eagle (formerly the Jolly Trolley) makes her winter home in Las Vegas and tours the nation during warmer summer months.

Star Ann got her start as a dancer in Phoenix, Arizona just about the same time as I did back in 1967. In fact, she was born and raised not far from Phoenix, in the town of Buckeye.

After high school, Star Ann moved to Phoenix and started go-go dancing. "My folks might have been shocked when I started dancing but they certainly weren't surprised. I'd been singing and dancing every chance I got since I was four years old. I just never got stage struck out of my system.

When I first started go-going, things were a lot different than they are now. You had to keep your top on! I also got to dance with a live band. I loved it. It was never work to me."

The blonde, blue-eyed dancer, 34-24-35, eventually moved to San Diego where she worked at the famous Body Shop. "I learned that pretty breasts and dancing go together. The Body Shop was my first topless job. Next door there was a strip club where they brought the Navy in by busloads. That's when I knew that stripping was my next move. I love the men! I enjoy seeing the desire in their eyes."

Star Ann invites you to come and see her at the Golden Eagle any night. P.S. She's never been married!

You'll be delighted with the rest of the dancing girls including Micky, one of the cutest dancers and best waitresses in town. You'll also be thoroughly entertained by the statuesque redheaded Muffie, exotic Lillie, Gay, Marty, Gail, Jane, Irene, and dozens of other equally gorgeous girls.

Harry Anderson, who just closed with Anne Murray and Larry Gatlin at the Riviera, got rave reviews. Harry is a superb magician with a dry repartee that both tickles and surprises his audiences. "Would you agree that this next trick is impossible?" asks Harry at first innocently and then with greater gusto and he gets the audience to reply yes. "You would? Then I won't do it!"

Stay tuned for more information on an upcoming 2AM and 4AM show at the Treasury starring Gale Baker former winner of Lounge Act of the year.

Be sure and catch magician-exotic Maria Del Rio at the Royal Las Vegas. Also appearing are **DI ALBA**, Sunny Day and Denise. The show stars comic-ventriloquist **LOU DUPONT.**

Did you hear about the banana-eating contest at the Satin Saddle in North Las Vegas? Comic **ARTIE BROOKS** gets girls up out of the audience for this funny idea and I'll leave to your imagination and curiosity to guess the rest. Nothing but clean healthy fun I assure you!

Vegas Visitor

1978 **MARILYN CHAMBERS** (pictured), X-rated films sexiest star ("Behind the Green Door") as well as America's innocent girl next door (Ivory Snow), has combined her substantial acting ability (rave reviews for "Rabid"), her sexy good looks (5'7", 114 lbs., blue eyes and blonde hair), in a one woman play "The Sex Surrogate" at the Jolly Trolley March 16, 17, and 18.

Miss Chambers, who plays several scenes in the nude and whose real life function is to dispel the myths and hang-ups that surround the subject of sex, will be holding a question and answer session on sex after the play.

The following are a few of the questions most frequently asked of Miss

Chambers in person and through her column in Genesis Magazine called "Private Chambers."

MARILYN CHAMBERS

What is your favorite fantasy? "I have a lot of them and I live them all out. I guess my favorite are submissive, bondage scenes with either a group of men and/or women."

Definition of frigid? "A woman not interested in pleasing herself or her man."

Has women's lib made a difference in men's attitudes towards sex? "Yes, it has made them more hung up, afraid to express their masculinity."

What puts you in the mood for sex? "I'm always in the mood!"

How did you get the role in "Green Door?" "I answered a classified ad in the San Francisco Chronicle. It didn't say what kind of film it was, just that it was a major film company. When they told

me the fantasy in the film, I knew I wanted to do it."

Did you see the film? "Yes and that turned me on too!" What is your ideal man? "Well he doesn't have to be good looking but I do like legs and of course the eyes, like when you see that certain gleam. The eyes tell it all."

Marilyn goes on to offer this advice to women who want to be good in bed. "Learn how to relax. That is the most important thing. It's sort of self-hypnosis. I believe your mind controls your body totally and unless your mind is into it your body won't be; then if you don't know how to let yourself go, you'll never have an orgasm. If you want to be kissed, kiss him. If you like back rubs, then give him one. Even if he doesn't return all your favors, you should get pleasure by giving him pleasure."

On the big "O." "There is more than one kind of orgasm ranging from mild shivery sensations to the really mind blowing ones."

In "Sex Surrogate," Miss Chambers plays the part of an assistant to a psychiatrist whose job it is to instruct patients on sexual dysfunction using a bright, optimistic outlook. She advises men to exercise to add longevity and variety to their sex lives.

Miss Chambers, who has appeared at the Union Plaza in the smash hit plays, "The Mind With the Dirty Man" and the "Owl and the Pussycat" with Barbra Streisand, will start filming again after she closes at the Jolly Trolley in an R-rated movie titled "Insatiable." The title carries enough sexy implications alone that readers can draw their own story line.

Marilyn has appeared in all the top burlesque clubs in the country always doing turn-away business!

Vegas Visitor

1978 "Boylesque '78" at the Silver Slipper is about to celebrate its' first anniversary and star **KENNY KERR** says, "We've had a lot of fun here and it looks like we'll be here another year."

What's all the excitement? "Boylesque" is a show with a little something for everyone, a chance to enjoy yourself while being treated to hilarious comedy in the person of **LIT'L LIL** (pictured) and strip-tease par excellence by Kenny Kerr with impersonations of show business greats like Judy Garland, Carol Channing and Barbra Streisand. There are several other female impersonators including Jan from the original "Jewel Box Review."

Throughout the show you are treated to glimpses of the most dazzling wardrobe in show business including a finale of beautiful boas created and designed by Lit'l Lil.

Kenny conducts a question and answer session with the audience giving them a chance to find out how old he is; 25. Is he married? Not yet, but he's looking. How long he's been in show business? Since he was 16. What his family thinks of him. They are all very proud. How long it takes him to make up? Twenty minutes. Is the blonde hair really his? Yes.

Kenny is working on a book during his spare time "an autobiography of how I got in this business." He's also preparing to do his first movie.

There is abundant comedy in "Boylesque" as Lit'l Lil frolics through "My Boy Lollipop" doing some amazing breast movements (difficult to describe but suffice it to say you will see his heart beat on both sides!).

He also does a cute black light number where you will see him "hiccup" with his belly button and make his "eyes" move back and forth.

My favorite comedy skit is still the Carol Burnett impersonation by Kenny Kerr as her Royal Highness the Princess of Monrovia. That skit alone makes the show a must see.

For fellow Keno addicts I recommend the Frontier Winner's Circle Lounge where you can try to make your fortune at Keno while enjoying the hilarious antics of the multi-talented Goofers (congratulations on your first album) formerly with Louis Prima, plus singer, musician Glen Smith (be sure and ask for "Piano Man") and the always superb Billy Kay. That's three shows in the lounge and all you have to buy is one drink!

The beautiful Gossett Sisters are back at the Maxim entertaining in the lounge with some brand new songs!

Like to jam? Try Sobella's where pianist, singer, composer Tommy Deering will accompany you as you sing or play. Tommy will also perform all your requests.

Vegas Visitor

January 1, 1979 The world is really very small and a recent addition to the Joker Club, Gina Adriann, is an illustration of that truth. Gina is from Phoenix, Arizona, which is where I started my career as a dancer. She told me she followed me into the Generosity Club in Scottsdale several years ago and she comes here from the HiLiter in Phoenix, which was one of my first jobs as a go-go dancer.

Gina commutes regularly from Phoenix to visit old friends so she doesn't get too homesick although she tells me she'd eventually like to work in California.

Romanticists will love this young lady when she portrays Scarlet O'Hara, the beautiful Southern heroin from "Gone With the Wind." Gina glides down the runway in a flowing ballroom gown of lime green which softly brushes those curious faces that might be trying to beat her to the number where she reveals a well-proportioned body under all that finery.

There is a new face in town **BOB "RUBBERLEGS' TANNENBAUM** (pictured) who just closed at the Cabaret and made a special appearance at the Sahara Showcase and possibly will be seen at the Jolly Trolley.

His unusual style of dancing combined with some comic antics might earn him the distinction of being a dancing Foster Brooks.

Bob likes to involve his audience and usually asks for a female participant who is hard-pressed to keep up with the agile dancer.

Bob has toured the world and even appeared at the 1968 Inaugural Ball for President Nixon. Known as "Mr. Discotheque," Bob combines a unique style, incorporating discotheque with acrobatically satirical jazz and comedy dancing. If you get a chance, go see him. You'll be in for an entertaining and unusual experience.

Vegas Visitor

January 5, 1979 Blue eyes is back! The marvelously funny and talented **FRED TRAVALENA** (pictured) is co-headlining with Shirley MacLaine at the Riviera. He brings to the stage a vast repertoire of songs and impersonations of show business and other greats including his most requested Frank Sinatra.

Fred is instantly likeable on stage. He has a boyish sincerity that comes through in his jokes and impersonations and he carries this sincerity offstage as well.

He is working on a special tribute to the great comedians and has already spent two years studying tapes and videos to get everyone down right. "If it isn't perfect, I won't do it."

The one he's having the most trouble with is Lenny Bruce. "Not too many people even remember what he sounds like but I do and I want to get it perfect."

Fred has been in show business ever since he can remember, first entertaining with his father Fred Travalena Jr. His dad and Frank Sinatra were fellow singing waiters in the 1930s and Fred III's life ambition was to impress Mr. Sinatra with his talent. He always brings the house down every time he does it.

Unlike many of today's successful comics, Fred disagrees that there are few places for a newcomer to get his start. He mentions the numerous opportunities to view the greats on television and the large numbers of small lounges, showcases, and talent contests.

"I think it was much harder in my father's time," says Fred. "He didn't have all the greats then that we have today to study from."

Fred didn't start out as an impressionist. He was a singer and a comedian. He won best singer in the Army. "I was really lucky there," he admits. "I was sitting around after the Viet Nam conflict just after Jack Kennedy was assassinated and waiting for my draft notice and I couldn't stand the pressure so I went down to volunteer for the draft. The guy had my notice on his desk all ready to mail out. By volunteering I got to take my pick of what I wanted to do and wound up in special services instead of maybe being a war casualty."

When Fred returned to civilian life, he went back to the small clubs and from there to a review in Denver. When it folded, he moved to Washington D.C. doing just about anything he could to make a buck.

He didn't seem to be able to get a break even though he worked at it every chance he got so he took a job for the Milton Paper Company in New York City where he worked for five years.

"They taught me how to work very hard for very little money! But I know that no matter what happens I've got a trade I can go back to. At the time I needed the day job for the security to pay my bills and on the weekends I worked every show I could get. My two weeks vacations I worked off-Broadway. I wanted to have my cake and eat it too."

It was fellow impersonator Rich Little who discovered Fred at Brickman's in the Catskills in 1971 and from there on Fred has done it all, including a part in the Buddy Holly Story, appearances at nearly all of the big hotels in Las Vegas, Reno and Lake Tahoe, plus his own television special, "The Funny World of Fred and Bunni."

And the offers keep pouring in. He's appeared on all of the major talk shows as well as the local television shows. He's been offered numerous game shows and commercials, which he has to date, refused.

"I call it socialized show business. The producers of the commercials are making a fortune and they are killing star statures. They pay a bare minimum, some don't even want to pay for repeats and all they talk about is how you'll make it all back in public appearances. I feel that if I am going to advertise a product then I should get more than the actor that no ones ever heard of. Instead, the producers are making all the money. For instance, the Hollywood Squares pays $750 a week and that's what they were paying in 1966. Figuring the inflation rate since then and the pay amounts to nothing.

Of course you have to have public appearances, so you just swallow your tongue and pick what you want and sound off like this when you have the opportunity. I confine my television appearances to the Tonight Show, Dinah, Mike Douglas and Merv Griffin."

Fred also reveals that he prefers to be the opening act for a female star unless the male is a super star like Ben Vereen. "I think you get a better blend that way. The men get to see the lady and the ladies get to see a man. It works."

He also states that he has little trouble with hecklers. "I just don't do that kind of show. Mine is more of a production show with the light and music cues. The audience wants to hear what I'm doing. They each pretend to be a critic. I can hear, "Nah, that doesn't sound like him. Yeah, that's right on,"

Fred is married to Lois James and has a one-year-old son Fred Travalena IV. His family, including his father, often accompanies him on his bookings. At home in Encino, California, he finds time to enjoy his family as well as do a little swimming, yoga, jogging and television viewing.

You can see Fred Travalena and Shirley MacLaine at the Riviera with show times at 8PM and midnight through January 7.

Vegas Visitor

January 12, 1979 Instituting a new show policy in order to give Las Vegas visitors a chance to see good entertainment nearly any time of the day is the Treasury Hotel & Casino (formerly the 20th Century) with two shows, "Topsy Turvy" and "Hollywood Follies." Topsy Turvy will star internationally known exotic Tempest Storm with a chorus line and several variety acts. Show times are planned for 2,4, and 6PM. The evening show will be "Hollywood Follies,"

which will star singer, impressionist **STEVE ROSSI**, along with the Susan Chambers Dancers, and several other variety acts.

Steve, who first appeared in Las Vegas at the Sands as straight man for Mae West, was half of the famous Allen and Rossi comedy team which played the country for over 12 years appearing on every major television show as well as starring in two pictures for Paramount, "Last of the Secret Agents" and

"Real Gone Girls."

Additionally, Steve was the comedy partner of Slappy White for some four years, making that team one of the first black/white teams to hit the big time.

As Allen and Rossi, the team put out 17 comedy albums with "Allen/Rossi Live at the Copacabana" setting a comedy album record of over two million in sales.

Steve Rossi has written a wealth of comedy material both for himself and for others including a book called *Final Daze*, a takeoff on the Nixon days. He is waiting for the April release of *The World's Funniest Sex-Rated Joke Book* published by Manor of New York.

He has also written several television pilots and some of the Carol Burnett sketches back in the days of Gary Moore.

Steve got his start as the 16-year-old star of both the Los Angeles and San Francisco Civic Light Operas in such productions as "Vagabond King," "Oklahoma," and "New Moon." "That made me light opera's youngest star in those days," says Steve.

He also had a nightly talk show with Don Sherwood out of San Francisco for more than two years. "It was like a Steve Allen show and we won every top award in television. Even though it was just a local show those honors meant quite a lot considering the San Francisco area has over a million inhabitants."

As a single, and as part of the Marty Allen team, and with Slappy White, Steve has appeared in every major hotel on the Strip including as production singer at the Sands which is where Nat King Cole first introduced Steve to Marty Allen.

Asked what makes a comedian funny, Steve replies, "The comedian must create the atmosphere. He must relax the audience and get them in the mood. Then it is the timing, the delivery that make the laugh not the joke itself, which explains why two people can tell the same joke, and you laugh at one and not the other."

Two of the comedians that Steve personally admires are Alan King and Jackie Mason.

Steve plans to make Las Vegas home and will move his family here from California this summer. When not busy working, he enjoys golf and tennis.

By the way, among the faces you will recognize in the evening show is lovely **PATTY WRIGHT** (pictured with Steve Rossi), who just returned from Miami and will be doing a special arrangement with Steve of "Send In the Clowns." In addition to dancing, Patty will lend a hand in the singing. "It marks my singing debut," she laughs, "I get to sing I am the clown!"

Vegas Visitor

January 1979 It's back again, the big question: Is nudity obscene? In the last few weeks several burlesque clubs in Las Vegas have been hassled, primarily by the news media, with so called citizens complaints about nudity as well as talk about putting bras on nude showgirls on the Strip.

Bearing in mind that each of the clubs post signs informing potential customers that their establishments offer nude entertainment and that such possible customer should not enter if nudity offends him, why a citizen complaint?

So it looks like, once again, someone may try to legislate everyone else's idea of obscenity. We can always recall former comparisons of the nude statues in front of Caesar's Palace, fine nude paintings, a multitude of girlie magazines, and the numerous adult book stores around town, not to mention so called escort services and their advertisements, but I'd like to go in a bit different direction and give my own definitions – my examples of obscenity.

I think people on the Gong Show singing off key are obscene.

I think $4.00 for a hamburger is obscene.

I think hemorrhoid commercials on television are obscene.

I think commercials touting the sexiness of cigarettes are obscene.

In the dictionary, there are several definitions for obscenity; disgusting to the senses, abhorrent to morality or virtue, or that which is designed to incite to lust or depravity. It is probably the morality of nudity that confuses. In morals as in all else, each person has their own standards. And going a step further to define a definition, lust is said to be pleasure, delight, a personal inclination or wish, an intense sexual desire. It has been argued that nudity creates lust. But apparently to many that which creates a lust for sexual desire are wrong and that which creates a desire to smoke is right.

Of course, there are many things other than nudity that causes lust depending again on each person's inclinations. When I was in high school, during the days of dress codes, girls were forbidden to wear floor length dresses as well as above the knee skirts. Both in their own way were said to create "distraction" in the male students.

Is a performance obscene because there is nudity involved? I've heard people remark on the "obscenity" of male ballet dancers wearing tights.

One thing must be recognized in entertainment. When a person must reveal their body in any degree to an audience, often openly critical, they tend to take great care to make sure that their body looks its best, no unsightly rolls of fat, no curlers in the hair, plenty of muscle tone, and often original breathtaking wardrobe.

As **TRACY SUMMERS**, exotic dancer at the Cabaret remarked, "More people should go nude in front of each other. Maybe then, they would take better care of themselves."

And as **BOB MITCHELL**, burlesque comedy star at the Maxim says: "These people are professional entertainers, putting a lot of time, money and effort in their work."

Obscenity is, I believe, a state of mind. You can see what you want in anything. No one looks at anything the same way. And just who is right? And further, does anyone have the right to dictate what is obscene. Should not our own conscience do that?

Vegas Visitor

January 26, 1979   Now in its 14th week, "Olde Tyme Burlesque" has established itself as one of the funniest, most entertaining shows in Las Vegas.

How can it miss with such a talented comedian as **BOB MITCHELL** with his sidekick, **CHARLIE VESPIA** and "Whistlin' Willie" portrayed by **TEDDY KING.** Teddy is also a straight man in the burlesque skits as well as the emcee and sound effects man.

And to these, add a bit of feminine pulchritude in the person of the dingy redheaded nurse **BRANDY DURAN**, and you're in for a night of laughter with such classic scenes as *the movie scene, the crazy house, trying to get arrested,* and *the transformer.*

Part of the uniqueness of the show is that no matter how many times you see it you will always have something to laugh at. The skits are never done like a script. Instead they are tailored to the audience. And, unlike some shows where there's a slow night and some of the best is cut, in "Olde Tyme Burlesue" you'll discover the skits get even funnier. Their secret? The ability to have fun as a cast. It's sort of like playing at home just for the family but the showroom provides an audience to share in the merriment. And many is the time when audience members can barely walk because their sides ache so much from laughing. Women should be cautioned to bring extra make-up for touch ups after the show.

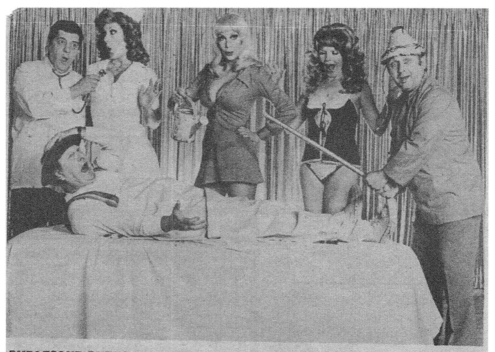

BURLESQUE BUFFOONERY — Now in it's 14th week, "Olde Tyme Burlesque", has established itself as one of the funniest, most entertaining shows in Las Vegas. Join funnyman Bob Mitchell with his side kick, Charlie Vespia, and also "Whistlin' Willy", Teddy King, Dusty Summers, Brandy Duran, and the one and only Angelique Pettyjohn. Join this delightful cast at the Allegro Lounge in the Maxim Hotel with such classic scenes as the "movie scene", "the crazy house", "trying to get arrested", and "the transformer". Showtimes are 8 p.m., 10 p.m., and 12:30 a.m.

And how do I know it is so funny? I have the privilege and pleasure of adding my own brand of insanity to the show along with exotic star **ANGELIQUE PETTYJOHN**. In addition to my own specialty number, I have a few lines in the skits and get a chance to share in the laughter and fun as does Angelique, who claims that since she's been watering Bob's petunias she's had dozens of offers to go into private gardening!

Pictured backstage at the Maxim are Brandi Duran,
Angelique Pettyjohn and Dusty Summers.

Vegas Visitor

February 2, 1979 **THE VELVET ODESSEY** (pictured) is back at the famous Palomino Club in North Las Vegas after a ten month tour which took her all across the country including Kansas City, Boston, Winston-Salem, North Carolina, and New York City where she auditioned and received the go ahead for a European tour this spring.

In addition to being an excellent exotic entertainer, as illustrated by a variety of imaginative acts including a belly dance show, a fire show, a Betty Boop show and others too numerous to describe, Velvet is also an ordained minister for the Universal Life Church and carries her ministry to the people she works with; in her words "the strippers and other sensual nightlife creatures."

Velvet believes in reincarnation and feels she has glimpsed edges of her own past lives during self-induced trances by concentration, visualization and meditation.

Velvet Odessey

She has studied theosophy (study of the Gods) since age 13, never feeling really comfortable in conventional religions so she searched for divinity and "found that it resides within each of us and the challenge is to bring it out."

Velvet tries to help others understand their karmic lessons in this life and the challenges each is faced with as well as making them understand that the standard Christianity is not necessarily the only path of Salvation.

She believes that "enlightenment can come from the dark downward path as surely as from the other path."

How do you join Universal Life Church to be a member of Velvet's congregation? Says Velvet, "It is not necessary to join. Being alive makes you a member."

Velvet also charts astrological signs and has been comparing them over the last couple of years. She finds that primary similarities are in the placement of Venus and the Moon.

"Strippers are often very dominating and independent women. They are usually very intelligent but undereducated as in comparison to their intelligence leaving them unprepared for careers that are not simply routine."

She has further found that there are lots of Sagittarian's and very few Pisces in burlesque. Velvet is a Sagittarian.

In her return to the Palomino, Velvet has brought back an additional sensual show, medieval in flavor and inspired by the Audrey Beardsley print "The Peacock Skirt." Accompanied by classical rock, such as Emerson Lake and Palmer as well as the Electric Light Orchestra and Brian Foley, you're sure to be entranced by this very lovely woman.

Magic lovers should be sure and catch Carlton and Co. at the Flamingo Hilton in "Razzle Dazzle." You'll see some outstanding illusions, some beautiful blondes, and some ferocious exotic animals, sometimes simultaneously.

Also, magicians, friends, and interested onlookers will enjoy the Wednesday night, from Midnight on, magic meetings hosted by **GARY DARWIN** and held at Pat's Chinese Kitchen.

Join me at the Maxim Hotel for "Olde Tyme Burlesque" starring **BOB MITCHELL** and **ANGELIQUE PETTYJOHN** and you'll see more magic with my first big illusions performed with my assistant **BRANDY DURAN** (pictured with me).

Vegas Visitor

February 9, 1979 What a crazy world! A hurricane in New York, a tornado in Los Angeles and eight inches of snow in Las Vegas! I can imagine a Chicagoan coming to Las Vegas to get out of the snow just to find he couldn't leave town because the airport here was closed due to snow!

And I imagine that snow country tourists were amused by Las Vegas residents as we ooed and aahed over each snowflake hurrying out to make, for many of us, our first snow ball and getting out our cameras to take pictures of the scenery. I loved it!

Like many of the tourists, entertainer **SAMMY DAVIS JR.** and his wife found that after closing at Caesar's Palace, they were unable to get back to Los Angeles so they were forced to stay over and decided to make the best of it by having a small gathering with the cast of "Olde Tyme Burlesque" at the Maxim.

With comic star **BOB MITCHELL,** emcee **TEDDY KING** and his wife, exotic star **ANGELIQUE PET-TYJOHN**, talking woman **BRANDY DURAN**, light girl Joann, and me and my husband, everyone was made comfortable in Sammy's elegant new suite at Caesars (he got a kitchen in his new contract). Teddy King got comfortable by acting as bartender!

It was an informal gathering with conversation centered on religion, the latest jokes, and lots of good-natured teasing of Sammy and by Sammy. He reiterated his enjoyment of spending his time with other entertainers and he and Bob reminisced over their long friendship. Sammy complimented Angelique

on her role in a Star Trek rerun just aired that afternoon.

Standing: Teddy King, Dusty Summers. Kneeling: JoAnn, Sammy Davis, Jr. Mrs. Teddy King, Brandy Duran and Bob Mitchell.

Unfortunately the cold weather has not been kind to everyone and friends are dismayed to hear that **JESS MACK** is in Sunrise Hospital with pneumonia. He is now out of danger and on the road to recovery, but his wife Dorothy tells me that he is unable to receive visitors. He would love cards from friends, which should be sent to his office at 1111 Las Vegas Blvd. S. and Dorothy will see that he gets them. Get well soon, Jess.

Vegas Visitor

March 30, 1979 Singer, dancer, actress, **ANGEL CARTER** (pictured with James Garner), now appearing at the Cabaret Burlesque Palace, puts on one of the most provocative and energetic shows in burlesque. This talented lady really knows how to dance and, with her extraordinary measurements of 38½D-24-36, the 5'6" brunette beauty has no trouble keeping her audiences attention.

ANGEL CARTER

With all the recent filming in Las Vegas, Angel has worked in most of them doing extra parts including the highly successful VEGA$!

PATTY WRIGHT is now appearing with **STEVE ROSSI** in "Burlesque '79" at the Holiday International downtown. She's really excited about working in the all-new showroom.

SHERRY SHANE at the Joker Club has put together a dynamite act as a spider! Along with some Vincent Price dialogue and some fantastic combinations of music including "Welcome to My Nightmare," Sherry has a most original costume with a cape of rhinestone spider-like bands and a dress that kind of weaves its way around her body. Sherry is among the former amateurs from the Palomino Club and has been doing a great job since she's turned professional.

Vegas Visitor

April 13, 1979 She's the "Lone Fox" or to her friends "Foxy" and this beautiful platinum blonde is now appearing at the Cabaret Burlesque Palace. A Cancer, Foxy is a well-proportioned 5'6" brown-eyed 35-24-35 former high school counselor for Auburn County in California.

When Proposition 13 cut out the funds needed for her job and hundreds like it, Foxy returned to the profession she used to put herself through college earning a Masters in psychology from Oregon State.

"I dropped out of school when I was 16 but I always wanted to return. I thought education was the key to the all-American dream. Since Proposition 13, I've applied for numerous jobs in my field but there's also hundreds of others applying for the same positions and so far I've had no luck."

Between her high school and college days, Foxy worked at a variety of jobs but she found go-go dancing paid best. She also took up exotic dancing working with **JAN FONTAINE**, doing private shows for Elks, Moose Clubs and the like. When she graduated from college, she came to Las Vegas at Jan's suggestion and worked at the Cabaret for a year before getting her job as a counselor.

"I really enjoyed my work. I worked mostly with youngsters who couldn't make up their minds about going to school or what they wanted to do in life. Mostly they seemed to have very little ambition, no big dreams, and no goals. They weren't inspired. Most of them hadn't been 25 miles from home and didn't have any desire to see the world.

The girls wanted to be housewives and told me how much they just loved to wash dishes and dust and that they didn't need an education. Of course, I couldn't tell them that there was something wrong with being a housewife and wanting babies but I found it surprising in this day and age to find so many girls who had no further ambitions. I feel like I had a false impression about what a good education could do for me."

Obviously Foxy is one of those intellectual blondes you seldom hear about, and her tastes in literature reflect this. She enjoys Taylor Caldwell, Hemmingway, *Psychology Today* and her favorite book was *Notes To Myself* by Hugh Prather. She found it "honest, contradictory, simple, direct, and explicit. It says what we all say to ourselves but can't put into words."

Foxy plans to "keep advertising her true self to the world and to seek out as many multi-dimensional people as possible for friends." She wants to expand her perspectives. "With the limitations and boundaries of roles, it becomes inevitable that we all become experts at games. We play to control others and unfortunately in many cases

we lose control over our own lives."

Her favorite music comes from Fleetwood Mac, Bob Seger, Peter Nero, and Janis Ian.

Her exotic style? Elegant, smooth, sophisticated, and waiting – for you!

Vegas Visitor

April 1979 You're going to have to hurry if you want to catch the dancing talents of Michelle Monet at the Cabaret before she leaves the world of entertainment for the nursing profession!

Michelle has been training as a nursing assistant so that she may eventually become a surgical technician, something she's always wanted to do and had studied for before she became a dancer, eight years ago.

Since then, Michelle has performed all across the country. In fact, our trails crossed once at the Surfside 7 in Ft. Walton Beach about four years ago. She's also appeared at such top nightspots as the Rathskeller in Ft. Wayne, Indiana, Downers in Gulf Port, Illinois, the Palace in Wheeling W. Virginia and the Vixen and Playgirl in Evansville, Indiana. She has been appearing at the Cabaret here in Las Vegas for over a year.

You'll love Michelle's shows. She combines softness and feminine grace as well as dancing expertise in a variety of shows expressing her Cancer/Gemini birth sign. With her blue-green eyes, long blonde hair, and her petite 5'2", 108lb., 35-22-35 frame, she looks every bit the delicate southern belle she

portrays in her "Dixie" number.

Michelle admits to being more than ready to retire from burlesque. "I find I cannot express myself properly for the audience to understand when all they want to see is 'tits and ass'. I know I can help people in the hospital either by comforting them or helping the doctor in their treatment."

When she's not working, Michelle enjoys the solitude of the desert where she can go just to think and be free. She also enjoys snow and water skiing and reading.

At home she devotes much of her time to her five cats, four Siamese and one black cat, as well as her collection of owls and cats.

Michelle likes challenges but is put off by people who take her for granted or read things into her that are not there.

She enjoys the music of Moody Blues, Cat Stevens and any singer or group that have a message in their music.

Right now you can catch lovely Michelle at the Cabaret. In a few weeks, you may feel Michelle's soft hands on your brow if you should have the fortune of being ill!

Vegas Visitor

April 27, 1979 If you like pretty redheads, then you are sure to love **AMBER CORDAY** direct from the famous Body Shop in Hollywood, California and now appearing at the Cabaret Burlesque Palace.

Amber was born in New York and raised in California. Along with her 34-22-34 measurements, she has a B.A. in mass communications and a minor in public relations.

While working her way through college, as a cocktail waitress in a burlesque house in Portland, Oregon, a boyfriend jokingly suggested she fill in for a dancer who was ill. "He didn't think I would have the nerve, but I did and have been doing it ever since."

One of the things Amber enjoys most about the burlesque runway is the freedom of doing her own thing, "my own choreography and my own choice in music." She finds the burlesque audience difficult to play to.

"They don't want to take you seriously as a dancer. You really have to make them respect you, but when they love you they really show it."

When Amber got her first booking at the Penthouse in Vancouver, B.C., she reveals she had b.s.'ed an agent with a story about how she'd been in the business for years so he booked her as a feature and her first night on stage her zipper got stuck and she had to rip off her dress very unprofessionally in front of the huge opening night crowd.

Amber is very serious about dancing. After touring Canada and the South Pacific, she gave up stripping and moved to Los Angeles to study dance. She got into jazz and ballet and performed in a few production shows and got some television work.

This Gemini is also a very ambitious lady. She'd like to have her own show with her name up in lights. She plans to become the best dancer and singer she can be, performing for a live audience or on television.

Amber confesses, "I'm happiest when I'm dancing anywhere, anytime. It's my life. I'm a performer at heart."

Vegas Visitor

May 4, 1979 "The Flower of the East," **LA LANEAH LEE** (pictured), Miss Nude Hawaii, is strutting her stuff at the Cabaret Burlesque Palace. Her "stuff" includes measurements of 34-22-34 at 5'1" and almost 100 lbs., with shiny auburn hair and a very outgoing Gemini personality.

In addition to being Miss Nude Hawaii, she was also selected Miss Super Fox in Milwaukee, Wisconsin where she started her career as a dancer. Of Eurasian descent, La Laneah was raised in Korea, Hawaii and Milwaukee.

La Laneah, who has been dancing since age one, enjoys creative dancing, Latin, Hawaiian, and modern dance and incorporates all styles in her exotic shows plus some unique contortions!

While in junior high, she received an art scholarship and still enjoys interior decorating and acting. She'd eventually like to get into acting and modeling.

La Laneah's views on ERA will delight many a male. "I think it's okay for those who think they are men, but I like to be everything a woman is supposed to be. My home is a castle with or without a man. I want it neat, clean and homey. I like to be dainty and treated with special care and attention. I don't mind being equal in those terms!"

Her ideal man is one who is "well-kept, laughing, and themselves. I like them tall and good-looking. I don't like wise guys or egotistical men. I like to make them feel important. I like older men, but not too old!"

In addition to her Cabaret appearance, La Laneah has appeared across the country, some of her favorite clubs being Cheetah III in Pompano Beach, Florida, The Brass Ass in Newport, Kentucky, and Skull's Rainbow in Nashville.

I took another trip to Phoenix on Fontaine Airlines (Jan Fontaine is pilot and owner and a dancer at the Joker Club). This time we checked out the go-go clubs including the HiLiter and the Camelback Lounge where we saw what must be a new fad, dancers wearing fuzzy short socks with platform shoes.

The best entertainment was in a club called My Place. We asked a customer there if there was any burlesque in Phoenix and he told us there were some clubs but that they didn't serve liquor and he suggested the Blue Moon.

Upon arriving at the Blue Moon, we checked out their display window where several Las Vegas exotics were advertised as appearing and then we walked up to the male cashier to pay our $4.50. He identified himself as the owner and told us we couldn't come in because it was against the law to admit unescorted ladies! After explaining who we were AND pointing out my publicity photo in their display case, we were still getting the same story so we left for a restaurant a few blocks away. A policeman was eating in the next booth so I told him about the incident and asked if there was such a law. He said no but we could be refused admittance for any reason. I wonder if it was because we commented too loudly on the display case? Oh well.

Vegas Visitor

May 25, 1979 Celebrating their 24th wedding anniversary are **CHARLIE** and **LEONA VESPIA** pictured with their eight children aged one year to 19 years in the Treehouse Restaurant at the Maxim Hotel. Charlie is one of the stars of the "Olde Tyme Burlesque" show in the Allegro Lounge also at the Maxim.

It is a treat is to be invited to Charlie and Leona's house for a get-together. This last Sunday, they were celebrating Cynthia's first birthday. And what a crowd of people especially children – nearly 30 in all!

Charlie makes the best pizza hors d'oeuvres. One of his other specialties is a champagne punch with strawberries – indescribable.

The hit of the party so far as the children were concerned was the goodies- laden piñata hanging from a tree in the back yard. Nearly every child had a chance to hit at the piñata with a baseball bat before it finally broke and the children scrambled for the pennies and candy. Just to show his prowess with a bat, Charlie gave it a final demolishing blow.

Some of the guests present included Eddie Fox, Mrs. Victor Silvani, Jack Bushell, Mrs. And Mrs. Roger Bushell and Margarita Bushell, Don Frank, Suzanne, Gina, and Nicole Younge, Linda Gallegos, Amber Campbell, Gina and Danny, Richard Jon Singer, Fred and Mayling Hoffman, Mr. and Mrs. Robert Lane, Steven Lane, Kathy Kennedy, Syd Stembridge, and Angel and Catherine Taber.

Charlie's beautiful family includes: Cecilia, 19; Tina, 17; Cathy, 13; Dina, 11; Toni, 10; Charlie, 8; Chris, 5; and the birthday girl Cynthia, one.

Daughter Tina is also employed at the Maxim in the Treehouse.

Vegas Visitor

June 1, 1979 Back in Las Vegas after a year's cross-country tour is the lovely **AMARETTA** (pictured), presently appearing at the Palomino in the daytime show.

One of the bookings she most enjoyed was the Golden Banana in Boston where she was originally booked for three weeks. "The club and management, Mr. Louie DeBella, was so nice that I ended up staying eight months."

She also attended the Barbizon Modeling School in Boston and then modeled feathers in Brooklyn, New York.

Modeling feathers you say? Yes, Amaretta is a very talented fan dancer. While in Boston she received a call from Mike Sperling, President of Silko Manufacturing in Long Island, New York, which just happens to be the largest feather company in the country. Amaretta was requested as a consultant and supervisor in the making of feathered fans for Las Vegas shows.

"As a fan dancer, I knew the fans had to be light and sturdy," explains Amaretta.

Using Amaretta's advice, Silko has made 28 fans for the MGM "Hallelujah Hollywood" show. And now Amaretta is an official feather distributor and also works with designers in the dress trade and for large shows. In fact, if you're in the market for fans, call her at the Palomino.

Amaretta is again taking lessons from Manfree Makor who taught her how to use the fans nearly two years ago. Although she is now quite a successful exotic, Amaretta wants to continue to improve.

She intends to make Las Vegas her permanent home. It's good to have her back and entertaining. Welcome home Amaretta.

Vegas Visitor

June 8, 1979   Long before he gained fame as the Unknown Comic, **MURRAY LANGSTON** (pictured), now appearing at the Sahara Casbar, had been in dozens of national television shows as a comedy actor, owned his own nightclub and wrote material for several television shows including the Gong Show.

Murray was writing on the Gong Show doing mostly one-liners for Chuck Barris and watching the line-ups of curtain closers when it struck him that he could certainly use the $250 paid for such appearances.

"A curtain closer," explains Murray "is not actually a contestant, just someone who brings the curtain down, adds a little spice to the show."

And when Murray suggested his idea of a brown paper bag and the unknown comic, Chuck Barris decided to give it a try. After his first appearance he was so well received that he's made more than 130 appearances since and now even guests as one of the judging panel.

Why the paper bag? "I was embarrassed to go on the Gong Show after all my television exposure but I needed the money," explains Murray.

Even years after the Unknown Comic became so well known, friends and acquaintances are surprised to find it was Murray. "Of course my closest friends have always known. And now there are even people doing imitations of me!"

Murray credits his nightclub in Los Angeles called Showbiz as one of the biggest influences on his comedy career. "In the two years I owned the club I had lots of comics and I learned from all of them." These entertainers included Kip Addotta, Johnny Yuma, Johnny Dark, and Jim Stafford plus dozens of others.

Originally from Montreal, Murray is a 34-year old bachelor, 5'11½" tall with brown hair and blue eyes, and still speaking enough French to thoroughly charm any lady.

Murray is presently considering a

number of television series including one called "Scared Stiff," where he would play a bungling detective. He is also busy writing his own sit com television series.

Murray opens his show as the Unknown Comic for the first fifteen minutes and then makes a quick change off-stage and into Murray Langston.

"The Unknown Comic is actually a character I've created," explains Murray.

Preparation for the character includes about four hours of cutting holes out of paper bags previous to each engagement. "I have to use a fresh bag for each show because part of the act is drinking through the bag and that gets it all wet,

"laughs Murray. Murray can claim one of the most unusual deductions as an entertainer . . . deductions for wardrobe including a large number of brown paper bags!

This is Murray's third engagement at the Sahara and he can see for himself that he is steadily improving. "I used to hit about 25% of the time, now it's a good 50% and more."

Be sure and catch Murray this weekend at the Sahara Casbar. For Reno visitors you can see Murray in the Sahara-Reno lounge July 2-19 and with Helen Reddy in the Sahara-Reno main showroom July 20.

Vegas Visitor

July 13, 1979   She's a singer, a dancer, and a comedian, all wrapped up in one delightful package named Joni Walker. You can see this redheaded, green-eyed beauty at the Palomino.

Joni has a sexy voice and her wisecracks are really a very well worked out comedy routine combined with the tease of an erotic exotic and a southern drawl that makes everything all right.

Joni is the daughter of a coal miner from Welch, West Virginia, which is where she comes by her enticing accent. Eventually the family of eight children moved to Annapolis, Maryland but the drawl moved too.

Joni has been featured all over the

country getting her start as an exotic at the Gayety Theatre in Miami and then starring for Eddy Mode in Cocoa Beach, Florida for whom she had previously worked as a go-go girl. "He knew I wanted to be a stripper so he sent me to Miami and I learned how there and came back as a feature for him before going on the road."

In addition to her dancing, Joni was a frequent guest on local television in Florida and did several commercials as well.

She is interested in real estate and would eventually like to quit dancing and sell real estate. "Selling is a natural," says Joni, "we do it on stage every day."

Vegas Visitor

August 3, 1979   Well folks, just finishing up at The Old Chelsey in Kansas City, Missouri, and this has been some week–both in and out of the showroom!

Had the pleasure of working with

some dynamite entertainers including emcee, female impersonator; K. C. Belmont, belly dancer **DEIRDRE ST. GEORGE,** Hawaiian lovely Ming Lee, and Kansas City's ever voluptuous, Misty Russell, a look a like for Jane

Russell!

K.C. is a very funny comic and does some great impressions of Herman Hermit's "Hello, Hello," and Millie Jackson's "The Rap" sometimes scaring the h--- out of a few members of the mostly male audience members as he gives them an extra wiggle!

Deirdre St. George (pictured) is an exotic belly dancer who has performed all over the world and you can plan on seeing this delightful redhead in Las Vegas this September.

Misty Russell, at a mere 21 years old, has already toured the country several times since the age of 15. Club owners reading this now may well be surprised! But now Misty is all legal and very grown up at 5'3" and 38D-24-36.

Ming Lee is a 4'11" Hawaiian doll. A Leo who is celebrating her 21st birthday, Ming Lee is billed as Miss Hawaii of 1978.

While in Kansas City I had the opportunity to see other great entertainment including the fabulous Harry Blackstone Jr. and his lovely wife with their enormous illusion show in the middle of Swope Park.

Also caught the Jewel Box show – a la Boy-Lesque with outstanding performances by Mr. Skip Arnold, Mr. Sandy Howard, and Mr. Renee, and a real live girl – Legs Diamond who did a superb striptease.

An unscheduled show was held in front of the Tender Trap downtown at the noon hour as a lady calmly shed her clothes and streaked down 12th Street!

See you soon in Nashville and Chattanooga.

Vegas Visitor

September 1979 Back at the Golden Banana in Boston by popular demand (her third trip) is the one and only **GEORGETTE DANTE,** former star of the Royal Las Vegas "Rare 'N Bare" show.

Georgette, so well known for her amazing strength and her exciting and terrifying show, has added another dimension to her dynamite appearances – MAGIC! She is doing a complete magic show with lots of doves and a bit of audience participation, which is the most important part to Georgette. As she explains, "What I really want to go into is comedy. This gives me a chance to use a microphone and kibitz with the audience. Eventually I'll just do the comedy."

As exciting as it may be to see Georgette lift 200lb. men in the air and whirl them around the stage, or blow hot fire three feet in the air, or pick pockets of unsuspecting volunteers, she is ready to shelve the whole show. "It is just too dangerous," she explains. "I'm always recovering from a pulled muscle, or a cracked leg from jumping over tables. I'm more than ready for a change."

Georgette has been busy putting her plans in action. She's already giving singing a try and has her own group Slaphappy, with whom she's booked several successful engagements.

What Georgette is really waiting for is the premiere of a new ABC show called "Big Al's Dogs" scheduled for release in the spring of 1980. "If that clicks, I'm in!" The show is a musically oriented comedy from the 60s, a nostalgia filled era that gave us the Beatles and countless other groups that have become legends. The show will use a lot of variety acts such as Georgette. She will help book other acts for the show. "There are a lot of good acts out there who never get a chance. The format of this show will provide that."

After Christmas, Georgette will be in New York City to do a commercial for Volkswagen. "I've already appeared in lots of movies, but now I'm ready to go after what I want instead of waiting for someone to call me."

Vegas Visitor

October 19, 1979 It's a place where fantasies come to life. Where Cinderella becomes a queen. Where Elvis is given his umpteenth life. Where feathers, rhinestones, sequins and fabrics in every color are lovingly molded together to turn out some of the country's best-costumed entertainers. It is **HEDY JO STAR'S** (pictured) in Boston.

It's a madhouse, as any custom-made clothing, high fashion showroom would be, with a clientele that reads like the who's who of burlesque as well as numerous other entertainers – including Carol Channing.

Many of the exotics appearing in my columns are wearing the latest Hedy Jo creations, including Patty Page, **GINA BON BON**, **LYNETTE LEAH**, **SHERRY CHRISTIE, KIM CHASE, HOLLAND STARR**, and hundreds of others.

Hedy personally supervises every fitting as well as the design of the costumes. She directs her seven employees each step of the way. She has been in the business successfully for fifteen years – although her experience goes back many more years in the world of burlesque.

As you can see from this photo, Hedy was a well-stacked exotic dancer and singer for 32 years and while backstage she started making her own wardrobe and sewing for others in the show.

"Tony Midnight really helped me a lot," admits Hedy. "In the beginning he taught me all I knew. Then I decided it was really fun watching costumes take shape and seeing them on the girls. When I quit dancing I took designing classes in Chicago and Paris and I'm always learning something new."

Exotics who come to Hedy get more than just breathtakingly gorgeous wardrobes. Hedy helps them in their choice of music, suggests a move that would go well, a new hairstyle for this, an additional hint on how to make the most of the show the girl may be putting together.

The costumes are indeed expensive, but you get more than your money's worth. Hedy stands behind her creations, ready to make everything right.

How expensive? Naturally prices vary according to what you buy, but some of the samples I saw included an Ann-Margret type costume heavily encrusted with bugle beads and rhinestones - $1000, an Elvis Presley costume $5000, and a costume made of soldered rhinestones (including a mini skirt, short shawl, and corset) $2500. Hedy's husband Buzzy makes all the rhinestone jewelry and handles the bookwork end of the business.

How important is wardrobe to an entertainer? A few Hedy Jo's are almost guaranteed to get you a raise. How do you show them to a prospective entertainment buyer thousands of miles away? Well, Buzzy is also a talented publicity photographer and will photograph you on the spot in your new finery, all in living color!

Is there anything she doesn't do? According to a telephone conversation I overheard from a prospective Halloween customer, she doesn't do cupcakes!

Vegas Visitor

November 9, 1979 Looking like she just stepped out of the pages of *Seventeen* is the lovely **AJA LYNN** (pictured), 5'8½", 36-26-36 with hazel eyes and gorgeous long sandy blonde hair.

Originally from Chicago, Aja has featured at top nightclubs and theatres across the country including the Oak Theatre in Chicago, the Gibson Girl in Fort Wayne, Indiana, and at the Harlow in Orlando, Florida. She's been brought back and held over frequently here at the Golden Banana in Boston (Peabody).

Aja Lynn

Her senior homecoming queen beauty is just part of her big attraction. The other is her variety of entertaining shows including "Frankenstein and His Young Bride Aja." I haven't seen this act but Aja credits the act for some of her most successful engagements.

What I have seen are most of her other shows including my two favorites a little girl show complete with pantomime to "Sister Kate" and pony tails and climaxing with the very apropos "Oh, You Beautiful Doll." I also enjoyed her roaring twenties shows with music selected mostly from "Chicago" the Broadway musical.

Aja makes many of her own costumes. Most though, are made by Linzy

Kay, a retired comedian in Kansas City, Missouri.

With her height and beauty, you would expect Aja to be a model and indeed she does model for Wilhelmina Models Inc. in New York City.

Aja also has that one quality that is probably more important than her ability to dance and that is stage presence. She's also a great tease! As she says, "I think stripping has lost its major key. The most important point in stripping is the tease and many of today's strippers have lost the second half of 'striptease.' I want to be the best in tease stripping, and it comes naturally for me."

Eventually Aja would like to dance in a Broadway show!

Vegas Visitor

1979 Congratulations again to **BIC CARROL** (pictured), once **again** winning Las Vegas' Costumer of the Year Award for 1979 for "Razzle Dazzle" at the Flamingo Hilton. Yes, this talented gentleman won the award last year too!

Bic is a multi-talented artist, dancing, singing, choreographing, and staging shows all over the country. He started in burlesque in Chicago in 1957 teaching girls to dance at the Riptide Club in Calumet City, Illinois. Then he went on to produce shows at the Gem Follies Theater. At the same time, he was learning costuming from Tony Midnight and teaching dancing.

Bic was off to Paris in 1960 to perform in a nude club called Chez Noir with two snakes given to him by Zorita. Upon returning to the U.S. he continued to produce his own revues and worked in road companies of "Bye Bye Birdie" and "Guys and Dolls."

He has noticed the gradual replacement of featured acts with go-go girls.

Says Bic, "they work for $15 a night. Only Las Vegas has kept burlesque alive. "

Vegas Visitor

November 23, 1979 Las Vegas comes to Boston again, this time in the form of beautiful **GAIL BOWMAN**, (pictured) formerly a showgirl in the Folies Bergere at The Tropicana. Gail brings her showgirl assets – 5'11", 34-24-35 – to the Golden Banana.

The blonde, blue-eyed California Miss was recognized early in life as "Best All Around Baby" in 1951 in Santa Monica. She has built on that promising beginning by taking lots of dance lessons including ballet, modern dance, jazz, belly dancing, square dancing, tumbling, tap, and folk dancing. She also had training in modeling and has worked for the Bob Drake Agency in Los Angles, for Bernie Lewis in Hollywood, and for Holiday Models in Las Vegas.

Added to her list of dance accomplishments are costume making, guitar, and conga drums. She also enjoys most sports.

While performing in Las Vegas, she made an appearance on the 1977 Jerry Lewis Telethon in the "Folies Bergere," can-can sequence. In 1978, Gail appeared on the TV Celebrity Bingo Show in the pilot for the Mark Hannibal Show and while on the road she made a radio commercial for the King's Lounge in Guam.

Gail spent two years in college at Berkeley where she pursued studies in human psyche, healing, religion and self-improvement. She wants to give mankind the benefit of her positive outlook.

"I'd like to put forth a decent effort toward communication and practices which help to improve the quality of life on earth from the deepest personal level to the infinite possibilities of the universal level."

Pretty heavy stuff, right?

Gail goes on further, "The world is the greatest group effort I have ever witnessed. Thank you for making it possible and a special thanks to all those who have had a part in its welfare and mine. Keep up the good work."

And Gail is certainly doing her best, putting on a dynamite variety of shows and lifting the spirits of all who join in her personally sex-citing shows.

Congratulations go out to **HOLLAND STAR** and Ron Glidden, united in marriage September 16 in Las Vegas.

MURRAY LANGSTON, "The Unknown Comic," has a busy schedule lined up. In addition to his frequent appearances at the Sahara, Murray is guesting on several television variety shows.

Vegas Visitor

1979 There's a gypsy working at the Golden Banana in Boston by the name of Spring Taylor! The lovely hazel eyed redhead with a trim 5'6" 120 pound 35-24-36 figure brings the capacity audiences to attention as she dons a colorful and authentic looking gypsy costume and whirls around the stage floor looking more gypsy and dancing more gypsy than anything I've seen in the movies.

Her training in dramatics and dance, including a variety of folk dancing is incorporated into her sexy gypsy show as well as into a variety of dances from six different countries.

She also performs one of the most sophisticated and sexy "stripper" strips I've seen in a long while, displaying an air of classy elegance coupled with movements of cat-like grace and sensuality.

Her wardrobe is designed to add a touch of reality to her shows with a sparkle of rhinestones for glamour – most designed by Spring and sewn by various costume makers including Hedy Jo Star, Manzo and Robin Wood.

Of her shows, Spring describes her approach as dramatic. "I treat them as little skits. I often use comedy, tongue in cheek, and a light-hearted approach. I've had training in Flamenco, Indian, belly dance, folk, as well as ballet and modern and I make use of these in my shows.

"I'd like to reach a more legitimate showbiz audience. And I'd like to see striptease come to be regarded as more of an art."

Spring holds a B.A. in Psychology and decided to wait before obtaining her masters. "I really felt I needed to know a little bit more about life before I began telling others how they should run theirs. And as time went on I also felt that psychology places too much emphasis on the negative, actually reinforcing people's fears. I'd like to see a more positive approach to living."

Spring is also interested in parapsychology, psychic development, the human potential and health. She'd like to do some research work in parapsychology.

Unmarried, Spring says her ideal would be to marry a wealthy European, settle down in a villa in Italy, and raise a couple of children.

Vegas Visitor

December 29, 1979 There's a bit of Gypsy Rose Lee performing at the Joker Club in North Las Vegas in the person of **JUDY TAYLOR** (pictured). This young lady has taken much of the original score from the Broadway musical "Gypsy" and combined it with her own dance ability, even adding some original ideas to give a legendary burlesque figure new meaning.

Julie got her start in entertainment by winning a $400 first prize for a disco dance contest in Aspen, Colorado where she was raised. From there she went to Pandora's Box in San Francisco, followed by a six month tour of the Northeast United States plus Canada, nine months at the old Guys and Dolls in Las Vegas and some time at the Crazy Horse here in Las Vegas.

In those three years, Julie has picked up a lot of confidence in her ability as well as extra training in other facets of show business. She's taking acting and voice lessons and is currently a fashion model with Universal.

She says that she expects to try some high fashion modeling with *Vegas Visitor's* own cover and *Playboy Magazine* photographer, Robert Scott Hooper.

As a model, Julie naturally loves clothes, "especially the very Vogue, Bazaar, Paris fashions. I love the chicness of European fashion where even jeans are worn with style."

Previous to burlesque, Julie had some interesting jobs including that of assistant to a rattlesnake milker. "I had to shoot him with anti-venom if he got bit. I also fed the snakes. We had a lot of rattlesnakes and boa constrictors."

She also worked in a pewter factory making jewelry. She worked for an escort service in Aspen, where she escorted tourists to the skiing slopes. "It was a real escort service, completely legitimate and legal," Julie emphasizes.

She was also the first lady DJ in San Francisco where she spun the sounds at Christous.

Julie enjoys being an exotic. "As opposed to go-go dancing, I think there is a lot more emphasis put on your performance."

Julie has a number of specialty acts in addition to her Gypsy show including what she describes as a "light hearted rendition of "Little Red Riding Hood."

The blue-eyed blonde is single and very discriminating in her choice of men. She has no plans for marriage in the near future but confesses that if the day comes she wants a man totally capable of taking care of her. "I want him to take me away from all this," she says with a twinkle in her eye.

Vegas Visitor

1979   There's lots of surprises in store for you in Holiday International's "Burlesque '79." The show stars Steve Rossi of the former Martin and Rossi comedy team and singer of the three million copy seller "More" and the beautiful **PATTY WRIGHT**, who has been a featured exotic all over the world.

The surprises start with the fact that this is a free show with drinks optional. The cast size of the show is small but the quality is top notch.

There are two dynamite dancers and two show girls (Patty doubles as a show girl). The music is lively, the lighting is good, the staging, and costuming terrific.

But you expect that in any Las Vegas revue.

The real surprises are two of the supporting acts. One is lovely Debbie Goldman, who does a knock out job on the Gloria Gaynor hit "I Will Survive." I was disappointed that was her only number. The audience was ready for much more of her beautiful full voice and spirited delivery.

The second surprise was a juggler. Doesn't sound like much? Well, you really don't expect that much when you hear "juggler." But Wayne Mortenson is much more than a juggler. He is one of the funniest comics I've ever heard and accompanies his amazing adeptness for the art of juggling with a steady comedy patter sometimes aided with straight lines from Steve Rossi. Wayne is as funny as the best I've heard and funnier than most!

Attended a nice party at Gene Marvin's plush apartment. There was plenty of conversation with the interesting folks from the "Vegas" series as well as some of my favorite magicians including **GARY DARWIN**, Daniel, and Joe Condon.

There was also a nice party held at the Palomino for comedy star and emcee **ARTIE BROOKS** who is still celebrating his 39th birthday!

I hear that the "Improper Bostonian," **SANDY O'HARA** is scheduled to open at the Landmark soon. You'll remember her from feature stints at the Holiday Casino, the Silver Slipper, and the Cabaret. Her husband Dave Hansen is the show coordinator and quite a PR man.

I think it is always a good idea to recommend those who have done a good job for you to your friends and with this in mind I strongly recommend A Fast Printer, where I've done business with owner Veryl Thyfault over the last four years. Not only is the service fast and reasonable but also it is very personal. Veryl's customers include Sandy Zimmerman, Gina Bon Bon, Larry's Lariat, Jess Mack, and countless others. He is located at 304 E. Charleston. Tell him Dusty sent you.

Vegas Visitor

1979   The most exciting magic show of the year "Excitement '79" recently debuted at the Aladdin and stars magician **BRANDON SCOTT** (pictured) The show combines lots of amazing illusions with the dancing talents of the Michael Darrin Dancers, and the original theatrical presentation of Brandon Scott, and the magical mime

Jeff Brown.

Brandon, originally from Mexico, spent years perfecting his craft and then attended the School for the Performing Arts in San Diego where he mastered the art of entertaining as an actor would. He comes across as a blend of Dante and the devil!

His producer, Daniel Heller, is a boyhood friend and while Brandon studied the theatre, Daniel concentrated on business and economics and then the two of them took off on a tour of Europe and the Americas, looking at several shows, gathering ideas for their own.

With the help of director John Thompson aka Tomsoni, The Polish Magician, and four full months of rehearsals, "Excitement '79" was born. The show has already played to rave reviews all over California, in Lake Tahoe and in Reno. They are scheduled to return to Reno this summer.

This show is different from many of the magic shows I've seen in that its main purpose is to entertain not to amaze although it does the latter just as effectively. Dance numbers are woven around productions of beautiful girls. Some of the routines look like medieval rituals. There are female assistants but instead of merely walking across the stage and handing the magician his props, the assistant becomes one of the props and the girls are an integral piece of the show as they demonstrate their grace, dance ability, and their own acting ability complementing Brandon and

making him look all the better.

It often amuses me to find a "star" that neglects to make use of the many talents of the rest of the show cast, which can only make the "star" shine brighter.

Brandon best describes his technique with one statement: "I decided there was much more to magic than just performing the trick. If I have to sacrifice a little magic technique in order to give a more entertaining performance, that is what I want."

In truth, his technique is smooth. He bewilders and entertains, and behind the devilish eyes is the trace of a smile saying: "This is for you."

Negotiations are presently underway for the next appearance of "Excitement '79" so when you see the name on a marquee, make it a must see and like me, you'll find yourself seeing the show several times.

Local magicians and magic lovers, attention! The magic club hosted by **GARY DARWIN** has been moved from Pat's Chinese Kitchen to the banquet room at the Library. See many of the town's top professionals every Wednesday night from midnight 'til?

Vegas Visitor

1979 Few newcomers to burlesque make the all-out effort of **ELECTRA 2000** (pictured) now appearing at the Surf in Revere Beach, Massachusetts.

The tall blonde beauty, a former fashion model, has put together a combination of **HEDY JO STAR** wardrobe, dazzling lighting effects, dynamite music, and all out promotion to make her one of the top attractions in Massachusetts.

Add this to her soon to be released Penthouse Magazine debut, and you

have a proverbial overnight star. In the business barely a year, Electra has devoted her time to striving for the best. Hard work and a more than sizable monetary investment have paid off. She's now pulling in the bucks of some of the best-known names in the business.

Electra makes her views on burlesque very clear. "The people are ready for a show, not just a go-go dancer, or some show that relies entirely on vulgarity but a show with a message, with class, and totally entertaining. That is the kind of show a man brings his wife to see."

And indeed, Electra is a beautiful girl, who has put a lot of effort in her presentation. Her movements are well synchronized to her music and her lighting effects add a lot of drive. She has succeeded in coming across as a very sexy lady.

Vegas Visitor

1980 The delightfully uninhibited Tamara Sinclair is now appearing in the daytime, all-star line-up at the Palomino Club in North Las Vegas. This green-eyed blonde (36-26-36) Libra is new to the burlesque world having made her debut at the Palomino just over one month ago. Previously she was a go-go dancer for one year at the Crazy Horse.

With the help of friend exotic Ginger Lee, Tamara put together enough material in one afternoon to audition for **PAUL PERRY** at the Palomino. Liking what he saw and recognizing her potential, Paul signed her to an indefinite contract.

Tamara loves to be sexy, raunchy, and a bit of bitch as she describes herself. She particularly enjoys the kind of music that is identified with being a stripper, songs like "Daddy," "Love For Sale," and "Hard Hearted Hannah" which she really acts out! She encourages her audience to join in the fun as she lets lucky runway customers undo some of her garments.

Never married, Tamara loves the single life and the freedom she enjoys. She spends a lot of time at Caesars Palace where she plays baccarat.

As to her ability as an exotic, says Tamara, "When I was in high school I was a majorette and I won a lot of trophies and also taught baton. I think that it gave me the experience of performing in front of an audience."

So guys the next time you're watching a half time performance on a football game, watch that majorette carefully.

She may be the next big exotic star!

GINA BON BON continues her successful stay at the Can Can on Industrial Road behind Circus Circus. This lovely lady was recently seen on a Home Box Office special with Red Buttons in "Burlesque U. S.A."

Enjoy go-go dancers at the Tender Trap on Flamingo Road just down the street from the MGM. You'll be greeted warmly by some of the best dancers in town including Jacque, Jan, Sabrina, Cheryl, Debbie, Stacy, Terry, Julie, Coco, Jill and yours truly!

MURRAY LANGSTON, the Unknown Comic, who just finished his engagement at the Sahara's Casbar will be seen February 4 on the Merv Griffin Show. In the weeks ahead, he will also appear on segments of Norm Crosby's "Comedy Shop." During April, catch Murray in "Easter Sunday," a monster movie, in which he plays a religious fanatic.

LYNETTE LEAH, "Baby Doll of Burlesque" has announced she is planning a spring wedding to a Canadian musician. Lynette is a favorite at the Cabaret Club here in Las Vegas and we all hope to see her back again. Meanwhile, congratulations, Lynette.

Birthday greetings go to Cynthia Vespia who recently celebrated her 21st at a party given by her proud parents Charlie and Leona. Charlie is one of the stars in "Olde Tyme Burlesque" at the Maxim Hotel.

Vegas Visitor

1980 During my interviews with hundreds of exotics over the last several years, the one club name I heard most often was the Golden Banana in Peabody, Massachusetts, just outside of Boston.

Seemed everyone was coming to Las Vegas directly from the Golden Banana or they were on their way. I always heard it was a great place to work. And you know what? They were right!

The Golden Banana owned by Louie De Bello is one of the biggest nightclubs I've ever worked in. With a seating capacity of 500, it does standing room only business (650) four days of the week and capacity business the rest of the week featuring a variety of original ideas as well as some of the old stand-ards.

Here's a quick run down: Monday is dollar night. Anything you want to drink is one dollar all night long. Tuesday is Limbo night. Volunteers from the audience are brought on stage to see how low they can go. The lowest wins a cash prize. Wednesday and Thursday feature an amateur strip contest preceded by a disco contest in which volunteers are teamed with one of the exotics and the audience vote by applause for the winning couple that again receives a cash prize. Weekends are devoted to the all-star cast of nine exotic dancers in the evening show and draws patrons for a hundred miles around.

All of this is in addition to a line-up of feature exotics starting at 1 PM daily. Oh yes, I almost forgot, they also serve delicious hot, and from experience, irresistible pizza for 50 cents.

I'll be introducing you to one of the lovely exotics this week with more to follow in the weeks ahead. But first a message to the girls at the Cabaret from **LYNETTE LEAH,** (pictured) now at the Golden Banana: She says to tell you all hello, especially Alexis. Lynette closes at the Golden Banana this week and opens next week at the Squires in Revere just a few miles from here.

One of the most popular exotics in the show is **KIM CHASE** (pictured). With her curly blonde hair, green eyes and 35-24-35 measurements on a petite 5'2" frame, Kim charms her audience with a variety of well executed and sexy dance routines performed in some beautiful Hedy Jo Starr wardrobe including a dazzling Ann Margret copy adorned in solid silver bugled-beaded fringe.

KIM CHASE

Kim, who majored in fine arts and modern dance at Western Michigan University in Kalamazoo, Michigan and then had more dance training at the University of Tennessee in Knoxville, is best described as a sexy jazz dancer with just the right touch of erotic moves.

Her stunning beauty and pixie-type personality caught the attention of Hee Haw producers when she performed at the Rainbow Room in Nashville and she was cast as a regular in the Hee Haw Honeys as well as an R. Altman movie.

Performances across the country including Detroit, New Orleans, and Chicago have kept Kim busy the last several years and now she has decided to settle in the Boston area. Like many city people, Kim confesses she has never lived in a house, only apartments and she plans eventually to buy a home where she can decorate and plant her own garden.

Kim wants to stay in Boston because she is planning a December wedding to a Massachusetts State trooper! But not to fear, lovely Kim plans to continue her dancing career and is booked indefinitely right here at the Golden Banana.

Vegas Visitor

1980 "Take me back to the good old days and let me be a part of a REAL burlesque show," dreams Mickey Rooney as he sets the scene for the newest hit on Broadway in New York City, "Sugar Babies." Also starring the fabulous Ann Miller, the play opened to rave reviews in October and should be around a long time. Tickets are sold out for weeks in advance.

"Sugar Babies" also features Sid Stone, nationally known for the pitchman character he created on the Milton Berle Texaco Show, Jack Fletcher the haughty announcer on the NBC miniseries "Presenting Susan Anton," Tom Boyd, Peter Leeds, and our own **JIMMY MATHEWS** (pictured). Jimmy knows more than 300 burlesque scenes by heart and has played with all the famous comedians, including Mickey Rooney's father, the late Joe Yule. Scott Stewart portrays the Juvenile. Ann Jillian, a beautiful blonde dancer, plays the talking lady.

The Specialty act is performed by Bob Williams and his dog, who doesn't talk, dance, sit up or roll over.

The show features several classic burlesque scenes including *Broken Arms Hotel, The Doctor is In, Little Red School House* and *Meet Me Around the Corner*. There are so many one-liners and double entendres, you'll need to see the play several times to get them all!

Song and dance numbers include standards such as "I Can't Give You Anything But Love Baby, "Don't Blame Me," and "On the Sunny Side Of the Street."

Ann Miller is an incredible singer and dancer who adds special sizzle to this nostalgic tribute to burlesque. With a chorus line, tap dancing, fan dancing, comedy and more, "Sugar Babies" is filled with the laughter and glamour of a by-gone era, brought back to life by a great cast.

A special thanks to Mickey Rooney and Jimmy Matthews for treating my daughters and me to seats in the second row!!!

Vegas Visitor

November 1980 Gale Baker is back in full force, promising to bring foot stomping fun at the Treasury Hotel every Fri. and Sat. at 2:30 AM and 4:15 AM opening November 21.

A nominee for Lounge Act of the Year, Gale has starred in lounges all over Las Vegas as well as top nightclubs worldwide. She's a much in demand opening act for main room performers including Rodney Dangerfield, Don Rickles and Jim Stafford.

Maybe you've seen her as Officer Carol Parker on "Vegas" or in other numerous television and movie appearances including the Merv Griffin Show.

Gale now brings her "Cabaret Hour" to the Treasury with such talented performers as Gypsy, Eydie Gregory, Allen Tremont and yours truly, Dusty Summers.

Gypsy, a multi-talented singer and comic has toured with Kenny Rogers and worked his own one-man act in Europe and the U.S. You can't pin him down. One moment you swear there are shades of Jonathan Winters and a second later, you're sure it must have been Howard Keal or Dick Sharon. Gypsy is a marvelously versatile performer who as he puts it "entertains!"

Eydie Gregory known as the "Bronzed Illusion of Beauty," starred in the world renowned "Jewel Box Revue". Audiences are mesmerized with Eydie. They clap, they cry, they laugh and they love it! Booming music and bawdy comedy are Eydie's forte and if you're out for fun, Eydie will show you where it's at.

Singing host for the "Cabaret Hour" will be the suave, talented, and very sexy Allen Tremont, a well-known performer in the Borscht Belt of New York state where he is loved for his savoir-faire and joie de vivre. Allen will greet you at the door and favor you with his vocal talents a la Tony Martin.

I will also entertain you with my combination of magic and exotic dancing and maybe you'll get a chance to be my personal assistant!

Vegas Visitor

1980 There is an ordained minister stripping at the world famous Palomino Club! **VELVET ODESSEY** carries her ministry message to the people she works with. Onstage, she carries a message of sensuality!

Congratulations to Richard Saunders, son of **JESS AND DOROTHY MACK,** on his recently released book, *The World's Greatest Hoaxes.* It has some of the most fascinating stories I've ever read. Put out by Playboy Press, it is now in its second printing. I am looking forward to Richard's next book, which will be on Allen Funt of "Candid Camera" fame.

And remember if you want to learn some burlesque gags (Jess Mack has an extensive library of them), or you want to buy a whole show or just one of the best acts in burlesque including Georgina Spellman ("Devil in Miss Jones"), **GEORGETTE DANTE,** Busty Russell, **CASSANDRA LEE,** or dozens of others contact the **JESS MACK** Agency.

A new concept in showcase entertainment is on the scene at the Tropicana Travelodge. Hosted by Johnny Ricco, performers get the benefit of guaranteed performing times, up-front advertising, and two working stages with Peggy Gerrara and Ricco singing and emceeing between acts.

A special VIP section for impresarios is provided along with in-house taping facilities. Shows are scheduled Tuesdays through Saturdays from 8PM to midnight.

Be sure and catch "Le Whoopee" at Joe Jilian's on Spring Mountain Road. The show stars Frankie Carr and features lots of talent with Gale Baker, **HOLLY CARROLL,** Tucks and Taps and the Shirley Freeman Dancers.

And don't forget me! Drop in and say hello Monday through Saturday at the Golden Eagle (formerly Jolly Trolley). My show times are 8, 10:30PM and 1AM.

Vegas Visitor

January 16, 1981   SILKI ST. JAMES (pictured), one of the most provocative and successful exotics in the country, is now appearing at the Palomino Club in North Las Vegas after recently closing at the Sahara Hotel in Reno where she was appearing in "Burlesque USA" starring Red Buttons and Tempest Storm.

Cable television fans may have seen Silki in several HBO specials including "Burlesque USA". Las Vegas fans have seen her at the Cabaret and at the Maxim Hotel in "Olde Tyme Burlesque."

Silki makes her home in Las Vegas and as much as she loved doing "Burlesque USA" she was happy to be home and back on her ranch awaiting the birth of a new Appaloosa, maybe two! "One is confirmed," says Silki, "and the other is a strong maybe."

While she was in Reno, Silki got the chance to work on a ranch there helping to break wild horses for the Bureau of Land Management. "I really enjoyed that," says Silki. "They were so scared of people. And it was so hard to reward them. They don't know what oats or barley or foods like that are. It was a great experience."

During the week of Halloween, Silki along with three other show members,

April Maitland, Karen Van Aru, and Cary, entered several Halloween costume contests and had a good time attending lots of parties.

"We were dressed as nuns," relates Silki. "We had the big hat they wear which we made out of cake boxes sprayed black and the black head covering and the big gold crosses. We were nuns until you got down to our waists. Then we wore black garter belts, stockings, and high heels!"

Instead of a bible one of the girls carried *Joy of Sex*. "We were the Sisters of Perpetual Indulgence named after a group of female impersonators in San Francisco."

SILKI ST. JAMES

Their garb won them second prize at the Gala Halloween masquerade ball sponsored by MGM at Imagine That. First place went to MGM!

"On Halloween night for the first time in five years gambling ceased at the Sahara," recalls Silki, with an impish grin. "We streaked the place, totally nude. It surprised the hell out of me that we didn't get arrested!"

And I doubt that the Sahara will ever be the same.

Vegas Visitor

1981 "Burlesque's Grand Ole Gal," **JACKIE DUNN** is the featured comedienne emcee at the newly opened Pink Pussy Cat, 1401 Las Vegas Blvd. S. Making fun in the best Bourbon Street fashion, Jackie Dunn comes to Las Vegas via New Orleans where she operated the French Opera House Nightclub and became known as the "Mistress of Bourbon Street."

In addition to hilarious comedy sketches, Jackie also performs her own version of the striptease, treating one lucky audience member to his own harem! You'll have to see it to believe it!

Jackie's family is known as "The First Family of Burlesque," and with her daughters, Honey West, and Barbarella and her sister Emerald Knight, she toured the country with her own review "Bourbon Street Burlesque." Now Jackie plans to settle in Las Vegas and in addition to her duties at the Pink Pussy Cat, she is preparing herself for a job in the hotel industry by taking courses at the community college.

Jackie is also into the world of psychic phenomenon and has both studied and taught classes to develop a person's psychic potential. "That's what I really enjoy," admits Jackie. "I give readings as well but when you get into that, too many people call you constantly trying to get you to make their decisions for them. A reading still gives you space for your free will and I don't make up anybody's mind or tell them what to do. I can only tell them what to be aware of. In teaching, I get a chance to help people develop their own psychic abilities. Everyone is psychic. It is just a matter of learning how to use it."

Be sure and catch Jackie Dunn 's delightful brand of comedy at the Pink Pussy Cat.

Vegas Visitor

1981   For those of you who are looking for an interesting lunch break why not try the all-new buffet with exotic entertainment at the Joker Club in North Las Vegas across the street from the Palomino. That's right, entertainment with some of the country's top exotics and a sumptuous buffet as well. Entertainment is continuous with more than ten lovely exotics providing the fun from noon until the wee hours.

This week's line-up includes **THE VELVET ODESSEY, TERRI STAR, CINDY MALLETTE** (pictured), **GINA BON BON, JAN FONTAINE**, plus several others and even an exotic attraction to serve you in the person of **LOVEY GOLDMINE**. And in the evenings you'll find burlesque comic **JIMMY MATHEWS** acting as your host and maitre'd. Be sure and say hi to lovely Marge, your redheaded bartender and Gary who will deal you a game of 21. And there are also lots of slots!

Casey Cole, in addition to entertaining patrons at the Ambassador Casino, has also been named Entertainment Director. Anyone wishing to audition may stop by to see him Monday through Thursday, 10PM 'til 4AM or Fridays and Saturdays 4PM to 10PM. Casey is always looking for new singles and duos.

The Charles Street Symphony with Laura DeValle is back at the Bingo Palace. They can't be beat for a relaxing and entertaining evening of superb music.

See **ARTIE BROOKS** at the Palomino every evening as he emcees the amateur nude dance contest. Artie is a master of comebacks and his audiences love sparring with him. And there are always lots of lovely contestants several of whom have graduated to the ranks of professionals and can be seen during the daytime show including Sherry and one of the lovely Playboy models, Terri Thomas.

Vegas Maverick

June 1981   Beautiful redheaded **TERI STARR** (pictured), who is now appearing at the Cabaret, is set to open May 25 at the Penthouse in Vancouver, British Columbia as half of a magic-burlesque adagio team billed as "A Love Affair with Teri Starr and Jim."

Teri, known as "The Heavenly Body" 38½- 24-36 has been performing her own specialty numbers all over the world. She's also appeared in several Universal and MGM pictures such as "Police Woman" and "Police Story" and a number of commercials.

Jim also has an extensive background in dance and theatre having appeared in many off-Broadway productions. He also worked as a choreographer for several dance teams and small dance companies. Dancing helped support Jim while he attended college to earn a business degree.

Now Jim has applied his knowledge to create new routines for himself and Teri with the assistance of renowned magic team Ran-Del and Dawn (rumored to be the stars of the new Strip spectacular entitled "Beyond Magic". One of their major shows will be a complete magic and illusion show, "The Hobo's Fantasy." Sound intriguing? Teri described it to me.

"Jim will be on stage dressed as a hobo asleep on a park bench and I will start rummaging through his pockets producing flowers, silks, and so on. From there we'll go into illusions such as the substitution trunk. It will be a show we can do either as a straight magic show or combining burlesque depending on where we are."

Other shows will include "Old Fashioned Girl" which is pictured. They also have a Grecian show with Jim playing Apollo, a French maid show and a hooker show with Jim as who else but the over-dressed pimp!

Teri and Jim are really excited about their new act. "Everyone has been such a help and encouragement to us. Every time we need something or someone, they're there. It's like it's meant to be and we have a very positive good feeling

about it. We know it is going to be a success."

Teri and Jim certainly have the background necessary to make a successful team and offers from across the country demonstrate the interest in their act. After Vancouver, they will play the Cabaret in Anchorage and then work their way east across Canada and all the way to Europe.

Good luck to Teri and Jim!

City Lites

NOTE: City Lites was an entertainment newspaper that I published in San Angelo, Texas. I also owned Dusty's West.

June 13, 1985 Appearing through June 15th at Dusty's West is acrobatic dancer **ANGELIQUE MARIE** (pictured). From Hollywood, California, Angelique is a unique combination of exotic and acrobatic dancer. Totally in control, Angelique executes unbelievable movements in slow, slow motion.

Trained in a variety of dance styles including ballet, jazz and tap, Angelique incorporates them all in her shows which include a Spanish matador act, a New York, New York routine, and even a little old lady comedy show. Versatility, imagination, color, and drama, you can't beat the excitement of Angelique Marie.

City Lites

May 15, 1986 One of the country's top exotic performers **AURA LEIGH** (pictured) will be appearing at Dusty's West May 12 -17.

Aura Leigh is no ordinary performer. Combining acrobatics, contortions, and somersaults with special show themes,

outstanding choreography, props, special lighting effects, and a fabulous wardrobe, Aura leaves the audience clapping and screaming for more.

Winning the title of "Stripper of the Year" in 1984, Aura has since performed in the top burlesque clubs in the country and it is "standing room only" everywhere she goes!

Showtimes for Aura are 5:30, 9, 11, and 1. Arrive early for a good seat and remember there is no cover charge.

City Lites

June 26, 1986 Currently performing at Dusty's West is internationally known Las Vegas showgirl **CYNTHIA LANE** (pictured). Cynthia is a talented performer with years of training in jazz, ballet, and tap.

Raised in the theatre, Cynthia performed in stage productions of such musicals as "West Side Story" (her favorite), "Oklahoma," "Bye Bye Birdie" and "Guys and Dolls."

At about age 18, Cynthia was approached by San Francisco agent Shelly Rae and asked if she might consider stripping. "One show and I was hooked! I love it." says Cynthia who has since performed in Europe, South America, Canada, the South Seas and Australia where she lectured women libbers on feminism!

Says Cynthia, "the very nature of the business requires independence and personal responsibility." Cynthia's definition of a truly liberated woman is one who is pleased with her womanliness, responsible for herself both physically and emotionally, capable of making decisions based upon her own priorities and free of behavior patterns socially stereotyped as correct for her status as a woman.

"There will always be those who feel that we cater to and perpetuate artificial images of women. It is to those people that I direct the question: Is it we who are enslaved by the sexual stereotype, or the society that supports our work."

This year Cynthia is in charge of the Second Annual Golden G-string Awards to be held at the Sahara Hotel in Las Vegas October 1-4.

"It is a strip tease contest with each performer doing about an eight minute routine but there's much more. There are various seminars planned to teach stripping, costume making, how to become a feature, stage make-up and more."

Special guests will include Erik Lee Preminger, son of Gypsy Rose Lee and author of <i>Gypsy and Me</i> and exercise star Richard Simmons.

A panel of club owners and agents will also speak and answer questions on various aspects of the business. Dusty Summers, owner of Dusty's West, will represent San Angelo.

Don't miss Cynthia's performances. Stunning costumes, great musical arrangements, personality and dance ability make Cynthia one of the most accomplished performers in the business.

City Lites

July 10, 1986 Opening July 28 and back by popular demand in her fourth engagement at Dusty's West is **HELENA DA VEES** (pictured), the little girl who "does it all.'

Do you want to see a western show, an Indian show, or perhaps some top-notch belly dance routines? How about a fabulous Polynesian or Spanish show, complete with gorgeous costumes? No need to book a dozen lovely girls. Helena can fill the bill on all of those requests and more.

Only 23 years old, Helena has already won the "Miss Nude Burlesque" title for 1985-1986, was chosen "Miss Dakota Harley Davidson," and topped it

off with "Little Egypt of Burlesque" when she was invited to belly dance at the Averoff Supper Club in Cambridge, Massachusetts.

Perhaps Miss Da Vees reached the highlights of her career when she won the title "Miss Nude Burlesque" on August 24, 1985, in competition with some 30 top exotic performers in the country today, at Viner's Pub in Onalaska, Wisconsin. Although she does more than 30 shows, she chose the Indian show for Viner's contest. "I wanted to do something different," she says, "and I knew nobody else would use this type of material."

HELENA DA VEES

Since then she has taken her tremendously successful repertoire to such locations as the Club Mary in Sarasota, Florida, King Carmichael's in Ft. Walton Beach, Florida, Ed Murphy's Club in Michigan and now Dusty's West in San Angelo, Texas.

Before becoming an exotic dancer, Miss Da Vees was an accomplished belly dancer and is still doing one of her famous belly dancing routines, now with a bit of a difference. The costume comes off at the end of the show for a finale Helena calls "the belly strip."

A bundle of energy, Helena is not idle when she's offstage. Her hobby is para sailing. She can show you photos of herself gliding 400 feet aloft at speeds up to 50 miles an hour. She also swims, takes jaunts on a motorcycle and is a great chef, known for her spaghetti dinners. In quieter moments she likes to read everything from best sellers to biographies, and is an expert on her idol – Gypsy Rose Lee.

Helena is good at horseback riding and when she wants a faster pace gets behind the wheel of a racy car. She plans to race **DUSTY SUMMERS** at the Wall

Race track during her engagement here.

An attractive blonde with a 36-24-35 figure, Helena is smashing both clothed and unclothed. She has more than $30,000 in wardrobe, lots of props, more than 100 tapes and she travels with professional lighting equipment and a light man to run them!

She needs it all for her Jungle show with the big snakes, comedy girl, space and cabaret show, her comic old lady show, her Elvis and roaring 20s show, her fan dance, her four rock and roll shows and more.

Her ambition is to be a modern day Gypsy Rose Lee and to own her own nightclub. Those who have seen her perform will agree that she is well on her way!

City Lites

September 4, 1986   Presenting a unique mixture of mirth and magic at Dusty's West is **PROFESSOR TURBAN** performing nightly. Professor Turban comes to San Angelo for his first appearance direct from eight years as a cruise director out of Miami Beach for such lines as the Royal Caribbean, the Sun Viking, the Caribe, the Carnival and others.

His cruise ship experience included the coordination and organization of all ship entertainment and activities and performing.

Professor Turban has also performed in most of the major night spots in the country including the New Yorker in Chicago where he worked as a close-up magician and bartender, the Royal Las Vegas in Las Vegas where he starred in his own long-running burlesque show and the Conover Hotel in Miami.

Slated for an indefinite stay at Dusty's West, Professor Turban will also be opening the club for a special daytime session of close-up magic at the bar.

Note: Turban I were divorced in 1978.

Gypsy Louise had a career in real estate until the economy tanked. She is now a licensed caretaker and lives in Henderson, Nevada. She performed for Burlesque Hall of Fame in 2012 and 2013. Grant Philipo staged, costumed and choreographed her BHOF shows! In 2012, Gypsy was backed by the Stage Door Johnnies and in 2013 by Rudalenksa.

After leaving the road, Georgette Dante worked in her parent's carnival float business and ran sideshows including burlesque and alligator wrestling. She moved back to Las Vegas several years ago and has been very active in charitable organizations, performing her magic shows all over Las Vegas. Georgette made her BHOF debut in 2012. She is putting together a company to produce her own movies.

Delilah Jones lives in Las Vegas. After she quit dancing she managed several of Paul Perry's nightclubs. She made her BHOF debut in 2013 wearing a costume from Grant Philipo's Las Vegas Showgirl's Museum. She just finished her autobiography titled: *From Nazi Germany to Las Vegas Stripper, My Life Without Regrets* by Delilah Jones aka Doris Gohlke. She is working on another book tentatively titled *Conversations Backstage.*

Gina Bon Bon lives in Henderson, Nevada and is an accomplished artist. After numerous BHOF performances, Gina gave her farewell performance at BHOF 2013. Grant Philipo staged and choreographed her extravagant show.

K.C. Layne lives in Las Vegas and works part-time in a convenience store.

She is also an accomplished artist and has had several successful art showings in Las Vegas.

Camille 2000 is the author of a spicy autobiography, *Cosmic Queen* by Camille Sands and is the owner of Cosmic Hog Pen Motorcycle Leather in Miami, Florida. She is also a member of Screen Actors Guild.

Angel Carter lives in Pahrump, Nevada and keeps active in her community by helping out her neighbors and friends.

Lovey Goldmine lives in Las Vegas and teaches dancing.

Susi Midnight retired from selling fine jewelry for J.C. Penney's. She lives in Las Vegas and is very active in her church.

Brandi Duran lives in Las Vegas and is a cocktail waitress for a local casino.

Carme lives in Florida and is still singing, telling jokes, and loving life!

Bob "Rubberlegs" Tannenbaum lives in Las Vegas. He sells toe rings and other items at swap meets and conventions around the country. He emcees and dances whenever he gets the chance.

Gary Darwin is holding magic meetings every Wednesday night at Boomer's in Las Vegas. He writes books and performs in videos on magic and comedy. He has included me in many of his works most notably in *Magic Autograph Poster Gallery* (1989), which is a collection of his caricatures of magicians over a twenty-year span.

The Great Tomsoni aka Johnny Thompson and his wife Pam live in Las Vegas and perform all over the world. Johnny also works behind the scenes with magicians such as Penn and Teller,

Lance Burton and Criss Angel.

Patty Wright lives in California and Hawaii. She has an online site under her adult film show name of Patty Plenty Please. It is http://www.pplease.com.

Big Fannie Annie lives in Las Vegas. She participates in the Walk of Fame portion of the BHOF shows every year. She makes boas and dusters for dancers.

Holly Carroll lives in Miami and sings in nightclubs in the Miami/Ft. Lauderdale area. She made her debut performance in Friday Night's Legend show at BHOF in 2012. She is the author of a spicy autobiography: *The Chosen One.*

Satan's Angel is living in Philadelphia. Angel can be seen in the documentaries: *Exotic World and the Burlesque Revival* and *Satan's Angel, Queen of the Fire Tassels.* She is an international burlesque performer.

Bambi Jones, 82 years young, lives in Henderson, Nevada and performs in community centers and retirement centers, lecturing on burlesque and kicking up her heels a bit in the process too. She is the author of: *My Journey, Burlesque The Way It Was.* Find her very funny video at: http://www.youtube.com/user/BurlesqueBambiJones

Kitten Natividad lives in Hollywood where she owns some real estate. She never really retired from show business!

She is a frequent performer at BHOF as well as in nightclubs and theatres all over the world. Her website is http://www.kittenklub.com.

Tempest Storm lives in Las Vegas. Retired from dancing after a fall during a performance for the BHOF in 2010, she still makes personal appearances for burlesque shows all over the world. She is busy working on a documentary *Tempest Storm: Burlesque Queen,* directed by Nimisha Mukerji. Read her best selling autobiography: *The Lady Is A Vamp.*

Sandy O'Hara and her husband, producer Dave Hanson, are celebrating their 47th wedding anniversary! Says Sandy: "Love him even more today than on our wedding day if that is possible. We still do our show *The Best of Burlesque* down here in Florida. We are a big hit with the fun loving seniors that find their way to the Sunshine state. We are blessed with good health and wonderful kids and grandchildren."

Bic Carrol makes his home in Las Vegas and participates in Burlesque Hall of Fame every year. He was recently given a special award by BHOF for his contributions to burlesque.

Those of us who live in Las Vegas get together frequently. Dave Williams took this photo at the birthday party given for me by Delilah Jones in 2013.

Pictured are SinSity Pearl, Angel Carter, K.C. Layne, Gypsy Louise, Delilah Jones, Tiffany Carter, Dusty Summers, and Lynda Batton.

PARTIAL LIST OF NIGHTCLUBS AND THEATERS
WHERE DUSTY SUMMERS HAS APPEARED

Airline Inn	Phoenix, AZ	1966
Airport Inn	Tucson, AZ	1966
Alaska Way Hotel	Burns Lake, B.C.	1981
Baby Doll	Amarillo, TX	1975
Backlot	Kearny, Nebraska	1973
Bar K Pub	Kamloops, C.	1981
Billy Barker Inn	Quesnel B.C.	1981
Bimbo Club	Witchita Falls, TX	1981
Black Forest	Huntsville, AL	1973
Branding Iron	Tucson, AZ	1974
Body Shop	Tucson, AZ	1966
Brass Ass	Newport, KY	1981
Brass Rail	Sunnyvale, CA	1971
Brass Rail	Penticton, B.C.	1981
Bat Cave	Hollywood, CA	1967
Cabaret	Las Vegas, NV	1976
Capers	Phoenix, AZ	1966
Capri Art Burlesk	Memphis, TN	1973
Camelback Lounge	Phoenix, AZ	1972
Cheetah	Milwaukee, WI	1972
Cheetah III	Pompano Beach, FL	1975
Chilocotin Inn	Williams Lake, B.C.	1981
Classic Cat	Nashville, TN	1979
Classic Cat	Salina, KS	1979
Club Juana	Orlando, FL	1976 & 1981
Comer's	Lexington, KY	1971
Cork Club	Merritt Island, FL	1971 & 1982
Dinner Bell	Portland, OR	1968
Downer's	Gulfport , MS	1973
DuMaroc	Desoto, IL	1980
Edison Hotel	Pittsburg, PA	1971
Encore	Rochester, NY	1971
Follies Burlesque	NYC, NY	1972
Flamingo	Dothan, AL	1975
Frank Gay's Marquee	Rockford, IL	1973
Generosity	Scottsdale, AZ	1973
Golden Banana	Peabody, MA	1979
Golden Eagle aka (Jolly Trolley)	Las Vegas, NV	1980 & 1981
Gold Rush	Washington, D.C.	1971
Guys and Dolls	Phoenix, AZ	1972
Hannah's	Savannah, GA	1975
HiLiter	Phoenix, AZ	1966-1968

Kismet	Los Angeles, CA	1967
Hubba Hubba	Honolulu, HI	1968
Inferno	Columbus, GA	1975
Jim's Candlelight	Lakeland, FL	1971
Joker Club	N. Las Vegas, NV	1977
Little Richard's	Columbus, GA	1981
Lucille's	E. Dubuque, IL	1975
Mary's Club	Sarasota, FL	1974
Maxim Hotel	Las Vegas, NV	1977
Miramar	Ft. Walton, FL	1974
National Hotel	Vernon, B.C.	1981
Old Chelsea Theater	Kansas City, MO	1979
Oscar's Redmill	Grand Rapids, MI	1971
Palace Theatrical	Wheeling, WV	1973
Palomino	N. Las Vegas, NV	1976
Pink Pussy Cat	Orangevale, CA	1967
Pink Pussy Cat	Rochester, NY	1971
Playgirl Cabaret	Prince George, B.C.	1981
Penthouse	Vancouver, B.C.	1981
Playgirl	Evansville, IN	1973
Playground	Great Falls, MT	1981
Primadonna	Newark, CA	1968
Rathskeller	Ft. Wayne, IN	
Revelstoke Hotel	Revelstoke, B.C.	1981
Rose La Rose Esquire Theatre	Toledo, OH	1973
Royal Las Vegas	Las Vegas, NV	1975
Roxy Nightclub	Lima, OH	1973
Sir Lounge	Waverly, IA	1973
Skull's Rainbow	Nashville, TN	1982
Squires	Revere Beach , MA	1980
Sonny's	Portland, OR	1968
Speakeasy	Little Rock, AR	
Stagedoor	Buffalo, NY	1973
Stork	Bossier, LA	1972
Stock Market Lounge	St. Petersburg, FL	1974
Surfside 7	Ft, Walton Beach, FL	1974-75 & 1982
Teddy Bear	Boston, MA	1972
Tender Trap	Phoenix, AZ	1972
Tiger's Den	Tampa, FL	1975
Torch	South Bend, IN	1974
Torch Club	Minot, N.D.	1974
Town & Country Lounge	Indianapolis, IN	1971
Trader Jon's	Pensacola, FL	1974
Treasury Hotel	Las Vegas, NV	1980
Victory Burlesk	Toronto, Canada	1973
Vixen	Evansville, IN	1973
Weavers	Columbus, NE	1974

Made in the USA
Monee, IL
08 March 2022

92469741R00122